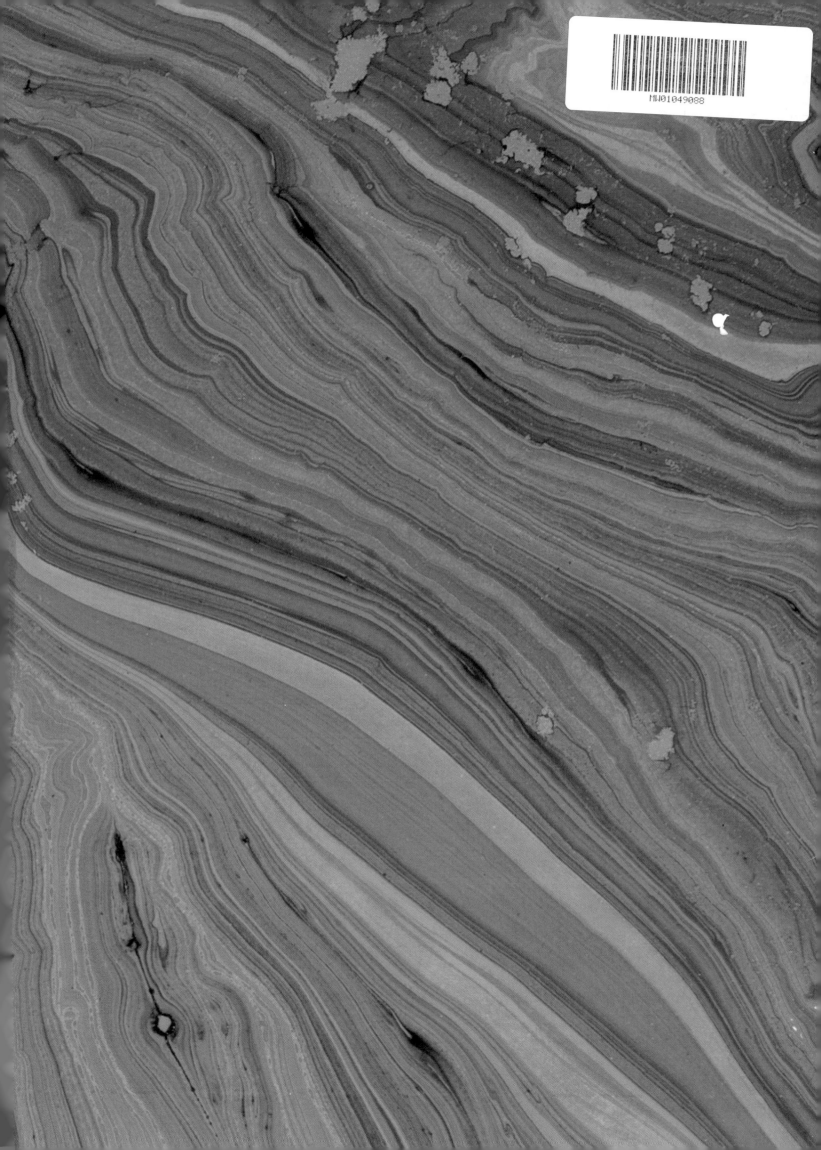

MARY MCDONALD INTERIORS

The Allure of Style

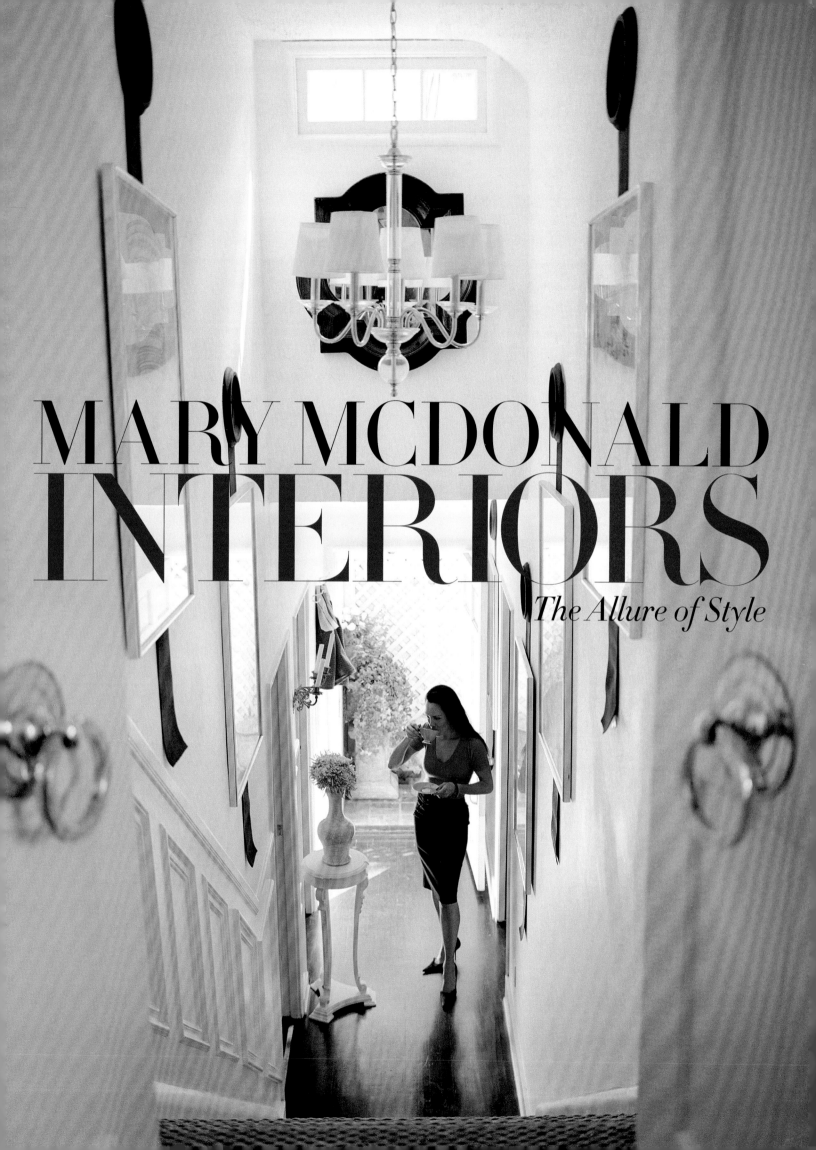

MARY MCDONALD
INTERIORS
The Allure of Style

In loving memory
of my
ever-encouraging
mother,
Marion Westenhaver
McDonald

INTRODUCTION

I grew up around stylish women. My grandmother was an incredible hostess, my aunt was a Brentwood decorator, and my mother was passionate about her artistic endeavors. These women all encouraged my creativity. When I was a little girl growing up in southern California, I swear I could not bring home a fabric-covered tin cup that my mother would not think was fabulous—and there was nothing quite so beautiful and brilliant to her as my macaroni collage paintings. I approach decorating with the same hands-on creativity that was instilled in me as a child. I love the production side of design. I like commissioning artisans to make furniture, lamps, beds, fabric bed treatments, and draperies. It's easier to have templates and buy name furniture, but it's more fun to approach each project as a tabula rasa. Even when I plan a room down to the last detail, I am always innovating and looking for new inspiration as I go along.

I didn't set out to be an interior designer. I left southern California to go to college in Boston, and eventually moved to New York and enrolled at the Parsons School of Design, where I studied fashion. I liked how fashion was constantly changing and open to experimentation and whimsy. I started making hats for fun, and suddenly hats were back in style. Designers such as Christian Lacroix were showing these over-the-top hats with their couture dresses, and real women started wearing hats in an exaggerated, fashiony, Hollywood way. I ended up on that express train as one of the hot young milliners-of-the-moment. I was only in my early twenties, and I was getting written up by *Harper's Bazaar*, *The New York Times*, *Vanity Fair* and *Women's Wear Daily*.

It was fashion that led me to interior design: My first client was the PR person for shoe designer Robert Clergerie who asked me to decorate her apartment because she loved mine. I had just returned to California from New York, and was living in a really fabulous apartment building on the border of Hollywood and Hancock Park. It was a chateau-like building, and my apartment was very "done." (Even when I was a student in New York, my apartment was fully decorated and done-ish.) The LA apartment was very glamorous for someone so young. It had a baby grand piano and all these wonderful oil paintings that I had taken from my mother's house in Brentwood. They were very good paintings, and I still have them. Since it was the 1980s, I had a few too many gilded things, but I thought it was fantastic.

The apartment surprised people, and it established my reputation as someone who loves drama, glamour, and bold gestures, which have become the trademarks of my career. I don't work by any one set of rules. I work mostly from instinct. Sometimes I need to cross the line to know where it is. While I am well versed in the technical and theoretical reasons why different colors and objects go together, my approach is visceral. My instincts are well honed, and, ultimately, I am always trying to create a sense of balance. Even rooms full of layers, multiple colors, and periods need to have a sense of balance. I don't mean necessarily pairs or symmetry. I mean aesthetic balance—an artful gestalt.

How do I begin a project? I consider the specific needs and lifestyle of the client, and then I assess the bones of the home in order to highlight the best architectural features and to fix the flaws (whether than means a construction project like adding a fireplace, putting in new windows, or raising the roof, or using paint or fabric to hide flaws). Then I filter the plan through my own reservoir of inspiration, which comes from so many sources: fashion, textiles, period clothing, old fonts, drips of water, peaks in whipped cream, old gold bullion, buttons, teacups, machinery parts, grasshoppers, lizards, animal furs, jewelry, rocks, minerals, leaves, flowers, the grain on an old piece of wood, the ridges on shells, black sand, bright plastic cups, Lucite, baby vegetables, fancy candies . . . my list is endless. My design work is an extension of my artistic soul, which also finds expression in cooking, gardening, painting, and fashion. Creativity is like breathing for me—it's my life force.

Over the years, I have lived in several houses, and I have come to appreciate how you can express different aspects of your personality in different homes at different times of your life. I like many styles—but I don't like them all together. It drives me nuts when people try to be all styles, periods, and influences at once and call it eclectic, which is often a catch phrase for I-don't-know-what-is-going-on-here. When I'm eclectic, I make sure that there is a strong thematic foundation so all the elements really do go together. While I'm a woman of many moods, charm and seduction are essential to my approach. A well-designed room should beckon you, make you feel welcome and wanting a little bit . . . more. I hope this book will make you feel that way, too.

—Mary McDonald, Los Angeles, January 2010

CHAPTER I

GREAT ROOMS ARE
SEDUCTIVE.
THEY BECKON AND EMBRACE
WITH THEIR FEMININITY,
SOULFULNESS, AND
DISTINCT PERSONALITIES.

When it comes to design, I'm an introvert and an extrovert. I believe that your home or office should express your taste and values. Sometimes you want nothing more than to create a space that's your own personal fantasia. But some rooms you want to share with your family and friends, and their pleasure and comfort become paramount. The eternal challenge is achieving balance, creating rooms that are dramatic but not overwhelming, sumptuous but not suffocating. A great room is as stimulating as it is soothing

My own houses and studios always have an allure. They reflect my sensuous, artistic side. I never play it safe—you always have a very clear sense of who I am from where I work and live. I need to surround myself with antiques, objets d'art, paintings, and photographs that fuel my imagination. Beauty is invigorating; it's essential to the human spirit. I can't imagine being as productive and buoyant as I am if I did not work from an office that is as carefully considered as my living room and bedroom. Of course, I am obsessed with design, but the principle applies even if you aren't as focused on decorating as I am. Your environment plays a big part in how you feel—and you should live in harmony with your desires.

There are countless ways for rooms to be seductive. My office, for example, entices me every day; it's an endless source of INSPIRATION that makes working a pleasure. I like a bedroom that feels FLIRTY, where you're as happy alone as when you're à deux. When a guest room has CHARM, it not only makes visitors feel welcome but imbues your home with a spirit of generosity. A little bit of WHIMSY goes a long way—there's nothing better than creating a room that makes someone smile. And if, like me, you think glamour is an aphrodisiac, then a DRESSY master bedroom suite is comme il faut.

PREVIOUS PAGES: Inspiration boards from the Mary McDonald Inc. offices.
OPPOSITE PAGE: I always like to have fresh flowers on the desk of my West Hollywood office. A silver sugar bowl borrowed from one of my favorite tea sets holds pink roses that are beginning to fade. A white murano glass vase holds green orchids.

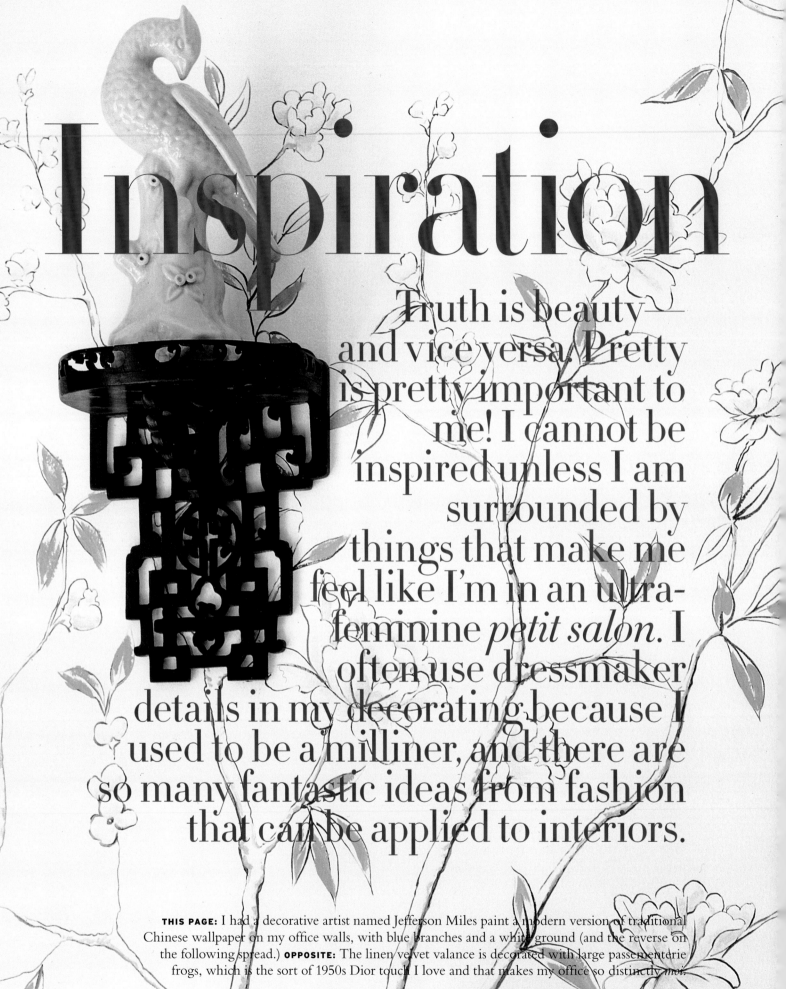

Inspiration

Truth is beauty—and vice versa. Pretty is pretty important to me! I cannot be inspired unless I am surrounded by things that make me feel like I'm in an ultra-feminine *petit salon*. I often use dressmaker details in my decorating because I used to be a milliner, and there are so many fantastic ideas from fashion that can be applied to interiors.

THIS PAGE: I had a decorative artist named Jefferson Miles paint a modern version of traditional Chinese wallpaper on my office walls, with blue branches and a white ground (and the reverse on the following spread.) **OPPOSITE:** The linen velvet valance is decorated with large passementerie frogs, which is the sort of 1950s Dior touch I love and that makes my office so distinctly *moi.*

I decided on a blue and white office instead of a pink one (my first inclination), because it was cool and easy and not too feminine, which might turn off male clients. Against blue walls painted with white Chinese branches by Jefferson Miles, I geometrically hung my eclectic collection of black-and-white fashion photographs—fine prints, postcards, and pages cut out of old *Vogue*s and a rare Richard Avedon book—in a manner I've dubbed "premeditated whimsy." The pair of silver-plated pagoda-style lamps is one of my all-time favorite purchases. I coveted them for a long time when I was in my twenties and worked for the L.A. antiques dealer Joel Chen. They cost a small fortune, but they were worth it because I still love them. They look perfect on the vintage Chinese modern desk that I found in some off-the-beaten-path shop in Palm Springs. Clients often flip for this desk, so now I make reproductions of it.

16

THIS PAGE: The closet doors had insets that were a perfect spot for bulletin boards. I had my wallpaper installer put painted cork inside the existing millwork, and then my upholsterer trimmed each panel with black grosgrain ribbon. **OPPOSITE PAGE:** I love the Chinese fretwork pattern beneath the desk's glass, but I rarely see it because my desk is usually piled high with files and fabric swatches, as well as beautiful things such as the large tray that holds just a part of my collection of reticulated silver cups. I like to use the silver for everyday items like paper clips and rubber bands, which dresses up the office.

Flirty

To be truly romantic, a bedroom must be playful. It can be chic as can be, but it must have a bit of "come hither" to it.

OPPOSITE PAGE: Before I used my Kings Road house as a guesthouse I used to live there. Nearly a decade ago, for my old bedroom I designed a bed with draperies and valances attached to the ceiling to create a dramatic, architectural bed treatment (without actually having to have a bed frame), which gives the room a formal dressed-up quality that is softened by the simple white-on-white piqué and matelassé bed linens.

THIS PAGE: The gilded bouillotte lamp had a black tole shade that I had painted gray to match the walls. I collect anything with a shell motif and the silver shell bowl with snail feet is one of my favorites. The pink antique Limoges dish belonged to my grandmother, and I keep it filled with muted hues of freshwater pearls and turquoise—I love waking up and seeing things I adore the moment I open my eyes.

My first impulse for any room is usually the color scheme: Here, I wanted deep gray walls and white furniture, which I thought would be soothing, feminine, and very Christian Dior. I added chair rails, moldings, and a mantelpiece to give the room a graphic quality that would be an enveloping backdrop for an assortment of glamorous furnishings such as eighteenth-century crystal sconces, a Venetian mirror, and a Louis XVI settee. I ripped out a wall of closets with sliding doors and replaced them with a fireplace. There's nothing more comforting and seductive than a fireplace in your bedroom. The 1960s painted Chinese coffee table holds dozens of crystal vases that I inherited from my mother and grandmother, which I hadn't planned on keeping. But then my friend Richard Sherman, a movie production designer, suggested arranging them this way, and I loved the idea because, well, I don't think anybody's ever done it before! Individually, the vases are sort of "grandma" but together they are compellingly contemporary and sort of "glamma."

Charm

Having grown up in Brentwood, the grandeur of old Hollywood speaks to me in a personally passionate way. The past must be respected, and the murals I found on the walls in one of my guest rooms of the legendary Mudd estate in Beverly Hills made me think of *A Streetcar Named Desire*—but with a happy ending!—and they set the palette for this ethereal guest room.

PREVIOUS PAGES: The room's color scheme of green, ivory, and muted silver was taken directly from the vintage mural, which feels like it came from the set of a Tennessee Williams play. I don't think guest rooms should feel anonymous; I think they ought to be faintly exotic. **THESE PAGES:** My inspiration for this bed came from David Hicks, the great jet-set decorator, though it's not quite what he might have done. It has a double-layered floating ivory pelmet whose shape is a riff on the curvy, ornate Italian headboard. The ceiling is painted the same light, peachy pink that's in the mural, which gives the room what I call a "glamma" look, which embodies the style of a super-glamorous dowager. Indeed, I can imagine Blanche DuBois living here if she hadn't fallen on reduced circumstances.

THIS PAGE: I have a fetish for chinoiserie: I can't resist anything with a pagoda or an umbrella, such as these porcelain candlesticks with the gilt tops. The antique doré bronze lamp that resembles a piece of coral inspired a design in my lighting collection for Robert Abbey. **OPPOSITE PAGE:** The original mural is reflected in the mirror hung over the skirted dressing table made of antique damask laced with gold thread and trimmed with square nailheads. **FOLLOWING PAGES :** I love the patina of the faded silver-leaf wallpaper in the bathroom, so I kept it along with the original 1920s gilded fixtures and coral-marble sink and bathtub. The faux bois gilded mirror was my addition.

Whimsy

I like things that are old school and elegant with a touch of whimsy.

PREVIOUS PAGES: A zigzag-painted floor adds zip to a sumptuous master bath that has a banquette with a waterfall skirt made from a Manuel Canovas gray-and-white–striped cotton. Painting is a good solution when you have wood floors and want to make a bold statement with a pattern. I like nothing more than the glamour of a banquette in a bathroom so it becomes a place to lounge and talk on the phone. **THESE PAGES:** This may be the world's most fantastic and romantic playroom, with its faux-painted tented ceiling by artist Maria Apelo Cruz. Everything is a subtle aqua-gray and white: the tone-on-tone slipcovers, the curtains, the playhouse, the linings of the baskets in the closets that hold toys and art supplies. I love how the scallop in the shades under the drapes matches the painted valance on the wall. Little girls love this room because they feel like fairy princesses here, and adults like it because they don't feel like they are stuck in a child's playroom.

THESE PAGES: The original black-and-white marble floors of the Mudd estate made me think of Ladurée, the fabulous Paris bakery, which became the starting point for my sweet yet sophisticated breakfast room. It's Dior meets Zsa Zsa, if you know what I mean, and I can imagine that Marie-Antoinette would have felt at home having a demitasse here. I certainly do. The funny, faux-French vintage chairs came with the house, and I had them lacquered the same gray-flannel color as the tablecloth; I decided that a rich gray was warmer than stark black or white. The layered window treatment includes curtains in a shell-pink cotton faille with a pleated valance, a striped under curtain, and black-and-white damask shades. The beaded crystal chandelier, which I found in Paris, indulges my passion for pagodas. If you blink, you would think you are in a chic French cookie shop.

THIS PAGE: The pink-and-green scheme of this ladylike little girl's room gives it a playful quality. I had the bed designed after a floating daybed at Chatsworth, the famous English country house. The pelmet is a striking bit of chinoiserie. The seating area is ideal for girl talk no matter what the age, or for reading bedtime stories. **OPPOSITE PAGE:** One of my favorite no-fail ways to keep rooms in balance is with a pair of chairs, which here flank the lacquered cabinet that hides the TV. The framed pagoda prints continue the chinoiserie theme while also providing symmetry and harmony.

THIS PAGE: For the Seaton boutique on Melrose Avenue in West Hollywood which sells high-style beach clothes, I chose an aqua-blue and gray theme that evokes the old-world chic of beach clubs with their changing cabanas. The all-shell grotto-style mirror behind the cash register was one of the old glamour elements that gave it a one-of-a-kind movie glam appearance. To give it a modern edge, I added over-scaled graphics of coral and sea life. **OPPOSITE PAGE:** I designed over-scaled cane panels for the windows, creating backdrops for mannequins without totally blocking out the inside of the store or the light. I hung them on contemporary chains from the ceiling. The geometric pattern around the tables on the floor mimicked the geometric pattern in the millwork on the custom cabinetry. Seaton-brand beach towels are displayed in painted terra-cotta urns.

Dressy.

I don't insist that everyone live glamorously, but once you try it, there's no turning back.

OPPOSITE PAGE: My friend Nathan Turner and I found a pair of nineteenth-century chairs upholstered with an eighteenth-century Aubusson in Paris. We agreed the pink and brown Chinoiserie motif was quintessentially me, and we had the chairs shipped back to California. **THIS PAGE:** I think of this as my "Jordan Almond" bedroom. It's an aqua-and-white confection that looks like a delectable cake, with its fondant millwork, moldings, and chair rails that I had a carpenter make for me. Aqua is my all-time favorite color. I wanted to have a girly paneled room in this house, the legendary Mudd estate, which has so many masculine paneled rooms. The marble fireplace surround was original to the room, but I added the mantel, which now holds an eighteenth-century reliquary. The painted mid-century starburst mirror adds a whisper of modernism. **OVERLEAF:** The color scheme was based on a bolt of vintage 1950s brown-and-aqua–striped fabric that I'd been dying to use forever and I decided that this was finally my golden opportunity. I had it mitered for the square pillows on the sofa. People tease me that it looks like I plan to have a board meeting here, but I believe that nothing is more luxurious—and, ultimately, practical—than a sitting area in your bedroom. The matelassé Ralph Lauren drapes and valance are trimmed with carved wooden bells and gauffrage ribbon.

OPPOSITE PAGE: The bed was based on a cabinet I saw in a book on Thomas Chippendale, and I added embellishments, as I often do, when I designed the bed with bamboo supports and carved finials. I had the coffee table custom-made with a sexy klismos leg. The footstool's graphic fabric adds a soupçon of seventies style that keeps the room from being stiff. **THIS PAGE, CLOCKWISE FROM TOP LEFT:** The flame-stitch wallpaper and patterned pillow in the dressing room are muted, complementary versions of the fabrics in the bedroom; part of my collection of *blanc de Chine* and Quan Yin figurines; a chocolate-and-aqua *houles* trim I use as a color-coordinated key tassel; the vintage bedside consoles were custom-painted because it's rare to find pastel chinoiserie—they're very theatrical and make me think of the legendarily outrageous L.A. decorator Tony Duquette.

I wanted the closet to have a lounging area as if it were an elegant dress salon from a bygone era. It has eighteenth-century chairs, a rock-crystal chandelier, and modern wallpaper that keeps it from being too old-ladyish. I chose not to put doors on the closets so that I could enjoy a sweeping view of my dresses and shoes. The evening bags are hung on hooks and arranged by color, beginning with pink and gold and then moving to silver and gray, black, green, and brown. The shoes are color-coded, too, instead of being organized by heel size. I always arrange my closets by color because it not only makes things easier to find, but also makes everything look more luscious and inspired.

50

THIS PAGE: I like to keep jewelry in the pink Murano ashtrays that I collect by the dozens. **OPPOSITE PAGE:** My dressing table has a wonderful provenance, and transports me to another era. It comes from the 1926 Buster Keaton estate in Beverly Hills, which was owned by Pamela and James Mason, whose daughter, Portland, gave it to me when I was helping to remodel the house. The dressing table was in terrible condition, and I had to have it completely refurbished, though I was able to keep its original hardware. The mirror I hung over it was crumbling at the top so I stuffed some feathers up there to camouflage the flaws. It's a tad showgirly, but it's amusing for a closet.

OPPOSITE PAGE: I painted the ceiling of the showhouse room the perfect pink that matches all the accents and gives the room a warm glow. The curtains on the window match those surrounding the bed. **THIS PAGE:** For a *House Beautiful* show house in Bel Air, I designed a canopy bed with draperies trimmed in wooden bells and hand-sewn ribbon trim that mimic the valance. A pair of Chinese Chippendale mirrors in a Versailles *gris* finish flank the bed. I usually put contemporary swing-arm lamps inside canopy beds for aesthetic and practical reasons: I like a touch of modernism even in the most traditional rooms, and reading in bed is one of life's easiest pleasures.

THIS PAGE: Contrary to my usual modus operandi, I left the wall behind the headboard bare to showcase the framed, antique de Gournay wallpaper panels on either side of the bed for this Beverly Hills bedroom. The aqua-and-*crème* color scheme is smart but placid with the washed-looking fabrics and Suzanne Rheinstein's elegant line of muted ikats as pillows. The ebonized furniture plays off the ceiling beams and ties this room to the rest of the very woody house. **OPPOSITE PAGE:** When there's a fireplace in a bedroom, it becomes a haven where you can lounge for hours, and this room is especially spellbinding with its gessoed antiqued Chinese table, crystal sconces, and watery curtains and upholstery.

I approach decorating a bathroom as I do any other room, and the lady's master bath in this hacienda estate is an extension of the boudoir in every way. The Gloria Swanson-goes-to-Rajastan mirror with the etched peacock is pure global glamour, and the Lefroy Brooks handset on the tub evokes a suite at one of the great old London hotels. A collection of antique Chinese vases and dishes all decorated with pastel colors coordinates beautifully with the adjacent aqua-and-*crème* bedroom. An ikat throw on the settee adds a note of worldly nonchalance.

CHAPTER II

YOU MUST BEGIN WITH WONDERFUL THINGS, BUT THE MAGIC HAPPENS WHEN YOU ARRANGE AND REARRANGE...AND THEN CURATE IT AGAIN.

If you're a born collector like I am, then you must think of creative ways to display the objects of your affection—whether you collect thimbles, pagodas, or enormous pieces of blue-and-white pottery, what I call MING bling. I'm not a collecting snob; I could start a new collection every day. I think you can mix pieces with various pedigrees as long as they are united by a passionate, considered eye. I love nothing more than seeing a curated collection of something I never found intriguing until it's been amassed in a particular and thoughtful way.

A well-curated room—whether indoors or outdoors—is breathtaking and eye-opening. It delights and astonishes, seducing your imagination by making you see things in a new light. A theme is essential, such as a modern MEN'S CLUB. It can be a feeling—a whiff of masculinity in every element that comes together to make you swoon as if you've just encountered the most handsome gentleman you ever imagined. Or a theme can be more quotidian—a celebration of greens, ranging from the wild majesty of pine trees to the sprite-like zing of spring buds. Though nature offers us endless greenery for inspiration, it's still a coup to create a VERDANT room that's fresh and original.

Austerity, as should be clear, is not my style. I'm always stocking up on FANCY things like gilded mirrors, sconces, antique lamps, *bureaux plats*, and silver candlesticks. I like to collect really superb antiques or iconically stylish pieces for my clients so that they will be dazzled every day in their own homes. I think comfort and chic should be synonymous. And though I am known for often being over the top, I do have a well-honed sense of restraint.

A cluster of blue-and-white jardinieres at my Kings Road property during its first incarnation. I would ceremonially drag my huge bone pagodas outside for garden parties.

Ming

Everyone talks about bringing the outdoors in, but I like to bring the indoors out. Why shouldn't your garden be just as glamorous as your house?

PREVIOUS PAGES: The gazebo I had built was my solution to the view of a dusty, useless hillside from the kitchen window of my Kings Road house in its first incarnation. I've used the gazebo as both an outdoor dining and living room. The all-weather drapes can be drawn to protect the eighteenth-century Swedish chairs, Chinese Chippendale mirror, and paintings by Clyde Scott. I had the checkered handkerchief cotton tablecloth made extra long so it would puddle romantically, and then placed a beautifully ironed white linen cloth on top of it. THIS PAGE: The brick-floored gazebo is set up as a living room with wicker furniture and a sea-grass rug. OPPOSITE PAGE: An all-weather synthetic rug that resembles sea grass defines an outdoor seating area at my first version of the Kings Road house, furnished with wicker furniture and pillows in Ralph Lauren fabrics. The two iron chairs, which I inherited from my mother, came from Greenacres, the legendary estate of Harold Lloyd in Benedict Canyon.

THIS PAGE: I chose a lattice pattern in stone and cement for the motorcourt to complement the gardens redesigned by Sean Knibb. **OPPOSITE PAGE:** The interior courtyard of the estate is breathtaking and architecturally stunning. **FOLLOWING PAGES, LEFT:** The original iron grillwork and black-and-white marble floors set the tenor for this vestibule at the Buster Keaton estate, which I furnished with an antique English settee that has its original needlepoint upholstery, an antique French rococo mirror, a gilded Italian lantern, and an eighteenth-century Swedish pedestal table. **RIGHT:** I had iron rods custom-made to hang atmospheric curtains on the back loggia of the Buster Keaton estate, which has English-style furniture upholstered in white canvas and blue-and-white Ralph Lauren fabrics. Fruit trees planted in antique blue-and-white jardinieres flank the sofa.

Men's Club

When my bachelor friend who has traveled the globe modeling and has a great eye asked me to decorate his house, I immediately thought of the late Bill Blass, the fashion designer who had impeccable, masculine style. Blass was never glitzy or over-the-top. His rooms were always muscular yet refined. So every step of the way on this project, the client and I would laugh and say, "What would Bill do?"

LAST HEROES

LOST EGYPT · VOLUME I·

THIS PAGE: The living room has the sensibility of an English gentleman's club, but with a modern flair. Antiques such as the nineteenth-century French urns and pedestals are mixed with new pieces such as the ebonized klismos chairs. Haberdashery fabrics provide a sense of well-tailored tradition. I used gray flannel on the armchairs and for the curtains, which are lined with vintage men's silk tie fabric.
PREVIOUS PAGE: An antique marble study of a foot rests on a stack of books in front of an eighteenth-century Empire *secrétaire*. The striped pillow in the foreground is made of vintage men's silk tie fabric.

THIS PAGE: A nineteenth-century captain's desk with a tooled leather top is paired with a gilded Regency stool in the bay window of Jason Shaw's house. Pillows made from vintage men's silk tie fabric enliven the English sofa upholstered in a white Rogers & Goffigon linen. On the wall, a pair of ebonized French mirrors and collections of red seals in frames flank the *secrétaire*. **OPPOSITE PAGE:** Jason is a serious chess player and we found this eighteenth-century chinoiserie board with extraordinary carved ivory pieces. The black basalt boar and curtains trimmed in vintage tie fabric have a strong presence.

I had the dining room painted a potent blue—navy mixed with a dash of royal. The eighteenth-century mahogany table and eighteenth-century chairs were purchased at separate auctions. The nineteenth-century French console is flanked by two nineteenth-century English turned-wood chairs upholstered in olive leather and a pair of nineteenth-century ormolu sconces that hold dripless candles. All of the prints on the walls are originals by Giovanni Piranesi, the eighteenth-century Italian artist famous for his etchings of Rome. To keep the room from feeling like a museum, I chose a shiny nickel chandelier from Restoration Hardware and a graphic jute rug. **FOLLOWING PAGES:** I forced Jason to have an instant silver collection for the sheer chic of it, choosing English, French, and American pieces that are decoratively stunning but also useful as bud vases, candy dishes, and ashtrays. This is the fun part of collecting, making a symphony out of disparate objects.

THIS PAGE: The dining room of the 1920s Vein house in L.A.'s historic Hancock Park neighborhood is a twist on traditional men's club style with deep blood-red walls and black lampshades on the antique continental chandelier and silver-plated lamps. I designed the ebonized pedestal table with claw feet and the upholstered chairs with the jaunty appliquéd racing stripes. **OPPOSITE PAGE:** A wing chair upholstered in black wool has an appliqué of braided trim in a whimsical Regency design.

THIS PAGE: As fastidious as I can sometimes be, I never mind someone whose bookshelves are so overflowing that he has to stack books on the floor, because I think it looks rather homey. The curtains are made of men's pinstripe suit fabric, and the front edge of the drape is done in a navy-and-oyster vintage men's silk tie fabric. The art is hung on gilded chains flanked by deer horns. A wing chair upholstered with gray flannel and trimmed in silver nailheads is pulled up to a contemporary sawhorse desk with a nickel-plated base and a crystal lamp.
OPPOSITE PAGE: I was on the verge of throwing out Jason Shaw's quite ordinary bookcase but then I decided to dress it up. It's a good example of how you can make a plain piece of furniture look stylish and chic by layering on objects such as shells, gessoed animal horns, a taxidermy bird, a collection of antique *blanc de Chine*, and a gilded column. I like to hang a big mirror or a painting on a bookshelf as long as it's not blocking something you need often. The custom English-style tufted slipper chairs are upholstered in white canvas.

THIS PAGE: This bachelor bedroom is seriously seductive. The back wall is upholstered in gray flannel outlined in nailheads to resemble paneling, which is hung with Piranesi prints framed in white-gold frames. The curtains are navy, and the gray flannel screen hides a minibar. The antique carpet is laid over a sea-grass rug with blue binding. A small convex mirror over the bed is flanked by antique Chinese calligraphy brushes. The pinstripe tufted-wool banquette has pillows made of men's silk tie fabric and a faux lamb throw.
OPPOSITE PAGE: The figure of Napoleon is an antique garden ornament that I paired with an English armchair and a pillow made of men's silk tie fabric.

THIS PAGE: A red-and-*crème* Brunschwig & Fils chinoiserie toile, which was used for the draperies and bed skirts, provides a clubby, English leitmotif for a guest bedroom at the Buster Keaton estate. I placed antique papier-mâché chairs with their original tufted seats at the ends of the solid, antique English mahogany four-poster twin beds.
OPPOSITE PAGE: I designed a new mahogany-paneled bathroom with a fireplace for the Buster Keaton estate that looks like it might always have been there. The opulent black marble used for the fireplace surround and sink in this portion of the bathroom was also used for the bathtub and walk-in shower.

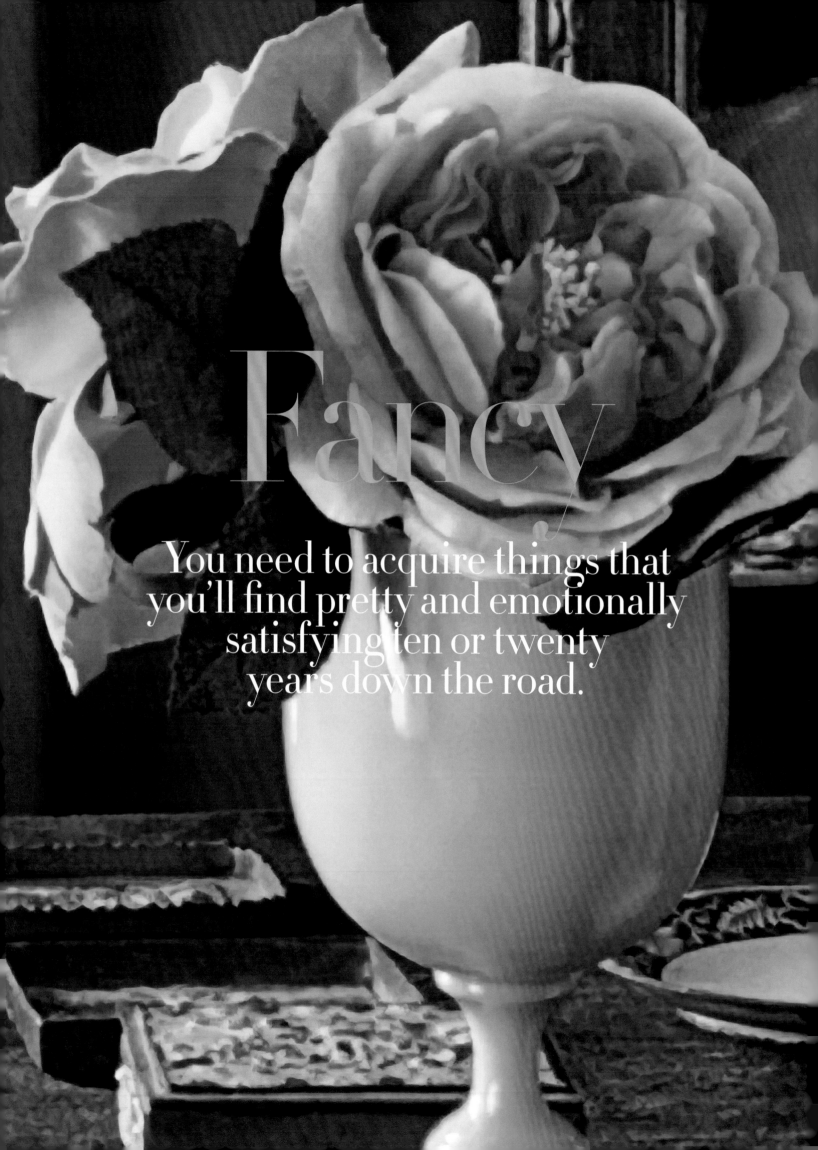

Fancy

You need to acquire things that you'll find pretty and emotionally satisfying ten or twenty years down the road.

THIS PAGE: I made an office for myself in what had been servants' quarters above the kitchen stairwell. It had its own attic with shelves and drawers where I could store my craft supplies, tear sheets, and fabric swatches. The room's genesis was a piece of Rose Cumming brown chintz that I'd been wanting to use for at least a decade. It's very old-school English with birds and flourishes, and I played off the colors in it. I brazenly painted the Chinese desk hot pink and gave it a European-style studded, linen-velvet upholstered top, which was inspired by the rooms at the Hôtel Costes in Paris where literally everything is upholstered—but I managed to satisfy my urges with just doing a desk. **FOLLOWING PAGES:** The room evokes an English country-house eclecticism that I associate with Cecil Beaton and eccentric fashion editors. I hung an odd assortment of artworks (including my nascent antique mother-of-pearl fan collection) with "premeditated whimsy." The cut-velvet waterfall skirt on the ottoman has a Duchess of Devonshire quality that amuses me and I need to be amused to be creative. The bright aqua garden stools and exquisite turquoise antique Chinese lamps contribute to the room's feeling like the inside of a candy box.

THIS PAGE: "Pretty in pink" is my mantra. I can make pink work anywhere, such as (clockwise from top left) a coral-pink study in Beverly Hills, an Anglo-English living room in Brentwood, a cinnabar vanity in Hancock Park, and a family-friendly living room in Brentwood. **OPPOSITE PAGE:** I used pink like a neutral for fashion designer Jill Roberts's home office, where I combined English, Chinese, and French antiques with a zebra-skin rug and a glam 1960s chinoiserie mirror.

Verdant

Nature gives us so many beautiful greens: Granny Smith apples, tropical frogs, grasshoppers, creek moss, and, of course, emeralds. But my absolute favorite is jade green, which always makes me swoon.

PREVIOUS PAGES: The antique china and famille verte Chinese vase were chosen because their flora and fauna complement the de Gournay wallpaper.

THIS PAGE: This jade-green, hand-painted Chinese wallpaper in the dining room of Jill Roberts's and Mark Freeman's home is emphatically elegant. The gilded nineteenth-century antique mirror and butter-yellow silk curtains help bring out the details in the wallpaper. The polished mahogany English pedestal table and ebonized Chinoiserie chairs are by Charles Fradin, who is one of the best furniture makers in Los Angeles. I had jade-green linen-velvet cushions made for the chairs. The nineteenth-century chandelier was found in Paris.

100

Green and brown are the most natural combination in the world (think leafy plants growing in rich soil) but you rarely see them in interiors, which puzzles me. For the upholstery, lampshades, and ceiling in my oak-paneled library, I used a mossy, lime green that feels like eternal spring. I mixed English and French antiques as well as fabrics that tied the room together.

FOLLOWING PAGES, LEFT: An allée of trees designed by Richard Hallberg outside the Harkham estate.

FOLLOWING PAGES, RIGHT: For my own dining room, I wanted to create a simple but soigné backdrop so that the table settings would be the main event. I chose a gray-and-white scheme that's an homage to Wedgwood with the chalky gessoed Chippendale chairs a sharp contrast to the drop-dead gray walls. Day or night, the splendiferous antique French bronze-and-ormolu chandelier is quite dazzling. Here the table is set with pieces from my extensive silver collection, which sparkles in such a chic, simple context.

THIS PAGE CLOCKWISE FROM TOP LEFT: Iron chaises in front of the allée of trees leading to the rose garden; one of the enormous antique iron urns that flank the steps to the pool; I transformed the pool cover into a chic beach with pillows and added antique wooden columns on either side to make an architectural statement. **OPPOSITE PAGE:** I placed a fanciful bench by Oscar de la Renta by the front of a wall of wisteria at the Harkham estate.

I like a master bedroom to feel like a lavish hotel suite with a generous sitting area for reading and hanging out. At a grand house in Hancock Park, I managed to juxtapose two stripes without the room looking as though it had been decorated by Lucy and Ethel. The interplay of greens—celery, moss, and lime—is balanced by the shiny black lacquered antique furniture. The graphic rug by Madeline Weinrib and Asian-inspired pillows give the room a contemporary sensibility.

THIS PAGE: Soft grays and lavenders work wonderfully with many greens, such as the lettuce-green-and-*crème* Chinese rug. The one-armed chaise of my own design is upholstered in a simple Silk Trading Company striped fabric. On the mantel, a 22-karat-gold-leaf mirror is flanked by English crystal girondoles.

OPPOSITE PAGE: I painted the inside of the antique French bookcase a soft gray-blue to integrate it with the living room. I designed the studded slipper chairs and had them upholstered in a favorite Lee Jofa chintz with muted silvery gray flowers (which I also used in the "Blanche DuBois room" on pages 26–31). The staid elegance of the silver urn lamp and mirrored coffee table are balanced by the playfulness of the Kathryn Ireland paisley on the sofa.

THIS PAGE: Painting the insides of the shelves lime green made them a stunning backdrop for a collection of white ironstone in this Beverly Hills breakfast room with black-and-white toile wallpaper hung above the high, paneled chair rail. Lime green pillows on the window seat pull the room together. OPPOSITE PAGE: A jewel-like opaline green lamp and Louis XVI chair upholstered in chartreuse silk-velvet linen are set off magnificently by an enormous, antique black-and-white map of Paris, affirming my belief that bigger is often better.

CHAPTER III

THERE IS NO FORMULA FOR
GLAMOUR.
IT COMBINES SHIMMER
AND CHARISMA.
IT'S ELUSIVE, BUT YOU KNOW
IT WHEN YOU SEE IT.

Having grown up in Brentwood, California, I am well versed in the Golden Age of Hollywood. My childhood imagination was colored not so much by motion pictures as by the great estates that were home to the greatest generation of movie stars. I often went to birthday parties at these astounding houses, which were palatial, romantic, and designed so their owners lived up to their glamorous personas. These architecturally rich houses had foyers, staircases, and doorways that guaranteed dramatic entrances—and exits!—and I suppose that's why I believe everyone should feel like a star in her own home.

Glamour comes in several varieties: I like it best when it's over-the-top and I can channel Ava Gardner and wear a duchesse satin ball gown at home—something I cannot really do on a normal workday! When I work on historic estates in Beverly Hills and Bel Air, I feel it's my duty to manifest their destiny and restore their razzle-dazzle. The architecture often points the way: a limestone loggia, a marble staircase, or a mullioned bay window can set my heart and mind racing. When there's inherent DRAMA in a house, I'm the director who wants to wring as much emotion as possible out of the scene.

But glamour, like the silent-movie stars, can be both subtle and INTENSE. Is there anything more CHIC than a French woman in a simple black dress and silk scarf? Chic requires editing and RESTRAINT, but when you get it right nothing is as bewitching. Ultimately, glamour is about romance and a love affair with your home.

PREVIOUS PAGE: The portieres create a dramatic sequence as you look from the foyer into the living room and the sunroom beyond. The yellow living room portieres were lined in persimmon velvet on the side facing the foyer. **OPPOSITE PAGE:** My love of glamour in decorating is only matched by my passion for fashion that dazzles. I bought this vintage dress, with the original Bergdorf Goodman label that says it was made for a baroness, at an auction. I am imaginative enough to be able to wear it around the house and feel absolutely appropriate!

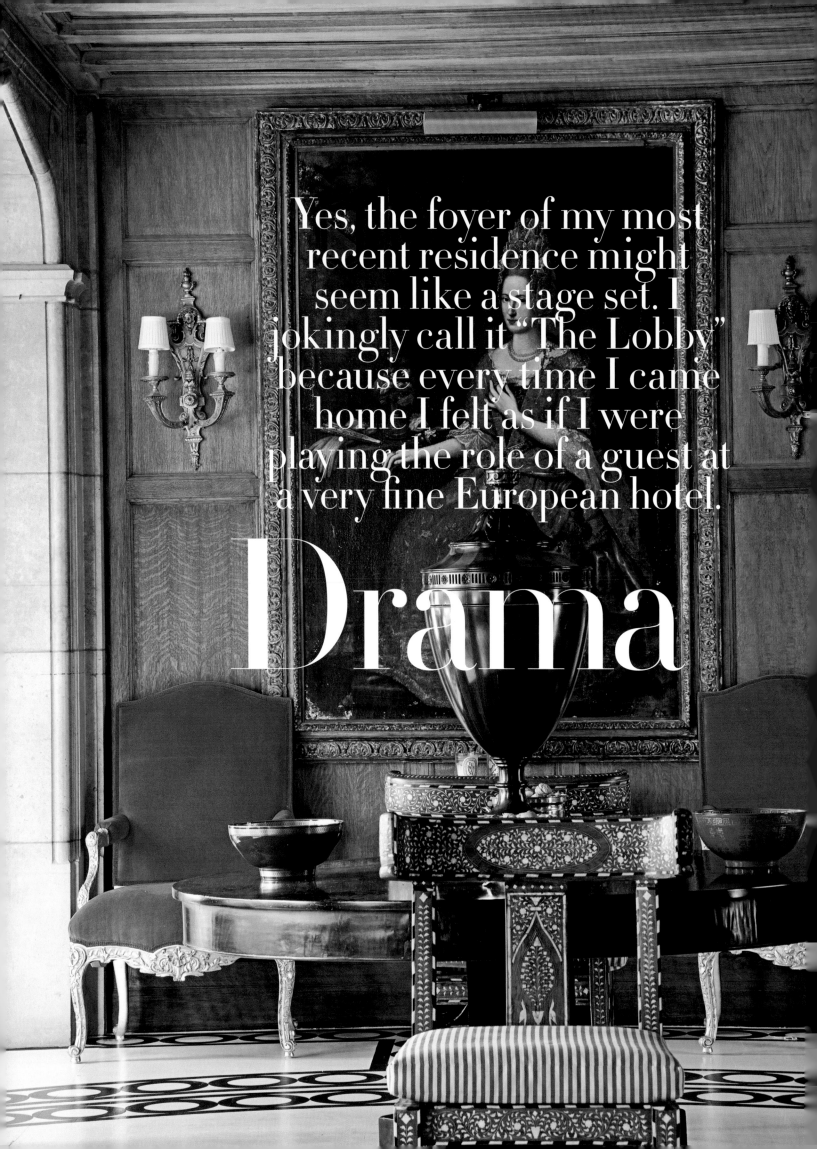

Yes, the foyer of my most recent residence might seem like a stage set. I jokingly call it "The Lobby" because every time I came home I felt as if I were playing the role of a guest at a very fine European hotel.

Drama

PREVIOUS PAGES: The original Gothic limestone arches are my favorite part of the entryway. I had to strip and bleach the paneling because it was just too macabre for my everyday life. I sparsely furnished the space so you could see the *crème*-and-ebony floor pattern inspired by one at a famous English estate. I chose a zippy persimmon for the drapes and upholstery, which seems to make the paneling look richer. I traded in the original patinated Tudor-style chandelier for a French cut-rock-crystal chandelier with enough pizzazz and height—it's nearly six feet tall—for the two-story space. THIS PAGE: In one incarnation of the foyer, I had eighteenth-century daybeds upholstered in cut linen velvet. The persimmon cotton velvet draperies are secured with brass Houles hardware and passementerie tassled holdbacks, which frame the view through the original bronze mullioned windows to the backyard fountain. OPPOSITE PAGE: A seven-foot-tall mirror that I bought in Paris and an oil painting from the Harold Lloyd estate lean on top of a table covered with a cotton ikat. The gilded stool from Joel Chen has a goopy, girly quality that helps keep the foyer from being too sober.

PREVIOUS PAGE: I wanted a formal living room that was not at all nostalgic but where women in gowns and men in black tie would still look absolutely at home. There are several seating groups, so it functions well for small or large parties. The challenge was to make it sunny without altering the original "Wayne Manor" paneling that I had waxed in espresso. I chose a refreshing combination of *crème*, lemon-yellow, and espresso for the fabrics, but the room's coup de grâce is the vintage chinoiserie screen, which evokes a timeless sophistication. THIS PAGE: Every yellow, gold, and white element in this room looks vivid against the dark walls, making this feel quintessentially Californian. One Christmas, I hung a garland of eucalyptus and lemons above my prized bone pagoda collection. OPPOSITE PAGE: I used gold accessories on the dark walls to bring shimmer into the room. The individual framed prints en masse are a map of the city of Paris.

THIS PAGE: This is the other end of my living room with my beloved collection of vintage pagodas. The original eighteenth-century versions were made of ivory, and many others are made of bone. I love how detailed they are, with little hanging bells and reticulated balconies with layers of faux millwork. I chose gilded furniture for this room because it's a wonderful contrast with the espresso walls. The vintage Chinese coffee table has a crackle lacquer finish and a modern silhouette that is refreshing for such a formal room.

OPPOSITE PAGE: The elaborate carvings on the mantel were reputedly done by Adam Dabrowski, the same craftsman who worked on the Fifth Avenue mansion that is now New York City's Frick Collection. Notice I never bothered to remove the nails I used to hang Christmas garlands and stockings over the fireplace. Every house—especially a lavish house—needs to have signs that it's actually lived in.

This is the garden you see through the mullioned windows in the entry foyer of the Mudd estate, with the original bronze fountain with the Three Graces on it. I love the original limestone and the balcony above the octagonal breakfast room.

THIS PAGE: A marble statue seems to gaze toward the slate-bottomed pool, which is flanked by two lidded stone urns. OPPOSITE PAGE: To balance the majestic pine trees and creeping fig that climbs a wall at the Mudd estate, I planted tailored hedges that beautifully set off the architecture.

130 INTERIORS

Chic

I want my rooms to have
an elegant aura and a timeless,
glamorous mystique.

PREVIOUS PAGE, LEFT: I used Paul Montgomery hand-painted chinoiserie wallpaper in shades of gray to make a screen that I paired with a *blanc de Chine* lamp for the Greystone Mansion Show House. **RIGHT:** A deep window seat becomes a refuge with silvery-gray Zoffany woven cotton-and-linen curtains hung on brass rods with crystal finials. The pillows and cushion were made in coordinating gray and silver fabrics. The overhead light fixture is a crystal pagoda I had made in Paris.

THIS PAGE: For this *Veranda* magazine Greystone Mansion Showhouse, I chose this room because I thought the millwork and wainscoting would seem very feminine painted a creamy semigloss by Farrow & Ball with the wall panels covered in a Phillip Jeffries ultrasuede. I wanted the room have the aura of an haute couture salon in Paris. To make the room double as a library or sitting room when no guests were in residence, I designed a daybed inside a low, modern tuxedo sofa. The Zoffany bed treatment hangs from the ceiling, which I had painted in graphic bands, giving it a hip modernity that contrasts nicely with the 22-karat flame-ball sconces that I designed. I love the dialogue between the fauteuils and the acrylic Allan Knight coffee table and the interplay between the hand-painted chinoiserie screen and the large-scale photographs of Moscow's Ostankino Museum by my friend Miguel Flores-Vianna.

134

THIS PAGE: A Maison Charles gilded-and-bronze pineapple lamp with a worn doré bronze-patinated shade stands on an eighteenth-century *bureau plat*. I designed the klismos chair with the classic Greek key pattern and hexagonal legs, which I frequently use in my projects. Over a black laquered chest of drawers I designed, I hung a large 1968 Henry Clarke fashion photograph of Valentino models at Cy Twombly's house in Rome, which evokes a cool, worldly sophistication that I try to bring to all my work. **OPPOSITE PAGE:** The walls of the dressing room are paneled in gray suede, and the rear wall is draped with pleated charcoal faille to hide a door to nowhere. I added a velvet inset to the acrylic Allan Knight vanity. The mirror hangs from ruched-fabric-covered chains, which makes it appear to float. A crystal pagoda chandelier hangs from the ceiling covered in silver paper from Phillip Jeffries. The dresses are from my personal collection of vintage couture.

Restraint

Restraint is the sister of chic. It should
feel like you're pulling the reins on a
bridle when the horse wants to gallop.

PREVIOUS PAGES, LEFT: Floors covered in glossy white marine paint with a charcoal border are inherently understated yet glamorous. They are especially inviting for a guesthouse. RIGHT: While symmetry may seem like the default mode for arranging furniture and objects, there is actually an art to combining pairs, as I've done here with the consoles, lamps, klismos chairs, and urns that are all centered on a 22-karat gilded starburst mirror above the mantel. I am so advanced at pairs I have moved on to collecting pairs of pairs!

THIS PAGE: Several years ago, I turned my Kings Road property into a guest house. The eighteenth-century *bureau plat* was an extravagant gift from a friend, and I need more friends like that! I like it paired with my lamp from Maison Charles, the legendary Paris design firm; I like how the shade and base of the gold pineapple lamp have a patina and now look like pewter. On the Chinese cabinet behind me, I have arranged disparate objects— kudu and gazelle horns, carved architectural fragments, and finely framed prints—in a collected fashion.

OPPOSITE PAGE: To make visitors feel they were having the full, sunny California experience, I painted the walls white, which give the space a loft-like feel. The enormous photograph of a Russian museum interior by my friend Miguel Flores-Vianna adds another layer of grandeur to the room because of its subject and size.

In decorating as in fashion, gray flannel is endlessly versatile. I like how sleek and modern it looks combined with bright white and raspberry. The calculated use of gold accents gives the room a regal aura. I added the antique mirror fireplace surround for an old–world effect.

THIS PAGE: Collecting is one of my obsessions, and I will collect only objects of a certain color for a time and once I have satisfied my craving I'll move on. During my green phase, I bought all sorts of antique and vintage vessels, including nineteenth-century Chinese, Moroccan, and green crackle vases from the estate of Tony Duquette as well as hand-painted vintage malachite obelisks. They made a striking vignette in the Kings Road dining room with a vintage Mark Shaw fashion photograph. OPPOSITE PAGE: This little dining room is visible from the living room and entry, so I used gray flannel to tie the rooms together, but used green accents and a gold-paper ceiling to give this room its own signature pizzazz. I love how the random crystals dripping down give the chandelier a romantic *Valmont* silhouette. I seem to be fine with anything if I can all of a sudden add a soundtrack and see it as a movie.

LE STYLE ANGLAIS 1750-1850

Christian Dior

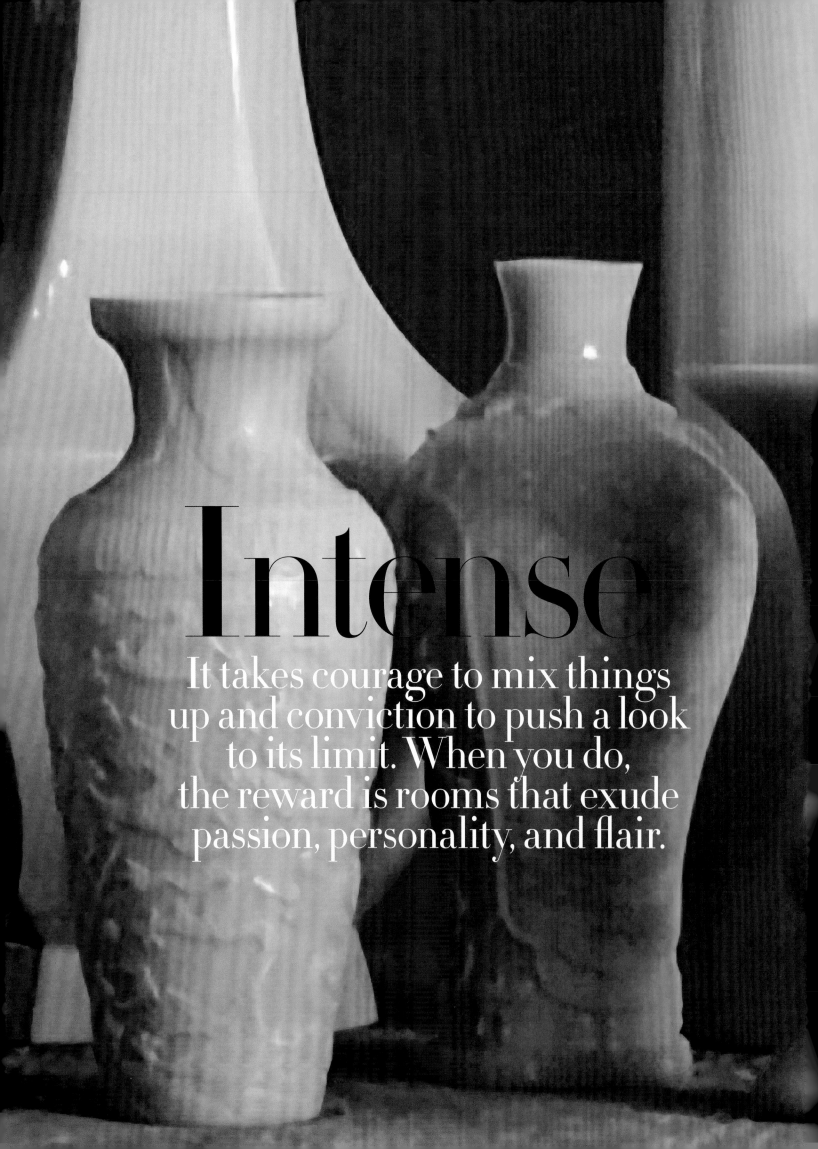

Intense

It takes courage to mix things up and conviction to push a look to its limit. When you do, the reward is rooms that exude passion, personality, and flair.

PREVIOUS PAGES: The foyer of the Harkham House in the heart of Beverly Hills has custom hand-painted de Gournay wallpaper that I tonally designed with bone-and-white trees that seem to be climbing the staircase covered with a sea-grass runner, which gives a casual California vibe to this formal space. The hand-painted graphic floor by Scott Flax is a surprising modern counterpoint to the French wallpaper, and the canary ceramics are a jolt of sunshine in the hushed setting.

THIS PAGE: The floors of the dining room, which are a continuation of the entry, were carefully plotted and scaled so there would be three sets of geometric patterns centered on the table and ending before the bay window. They complement a Robert Motherwell painting that is not seen in the photograph. The elegant pedestal table and leggy Charles Fradin sideboard allow the floor to be fully appreciated. The nineteenth-century chandelier is Russian, and the Louis XVI–style armchairs upholstered in black leather with nailhead trim are my own MMI design.

150

PREVIOUS PAGES: The loggia is really an outdoor living room, and it can be glimpsed from several interior rooms so it had to be aesthetically connected to the house. Zinc urns on zinc pedestals flank the entrance to the dining room. The outdoor furniture is a beautifully patinated cast bronze by Murray's Iron Works that is made to look like twigs. The slate tile floor and pewter-gray curtains contribute to the soothing, seductive mood.
THIS PAGE: As long as they are equally intense, you can pair dissimilar elements for a powerful effect, such as an eighteenth-century gilded settee with contemporary black-and-white photographs by Vicente Wolf, the esteemed New York interior designer. **OPPOSITE PAGE:** A console table decorated with gray shells and a wall-scape of contemporary mirrors adds a dramatic flourish to the Beverly Hills mansion.

PREVIOUS PAGES: When a client has a great art collection, you need to choose colors that will complement the paintings (though you never want it to feel matchy-matchy.) The watery shade of blue that dominates the living room was pulled from one of the clients' paintings. The room is almost monochromatic so that the furnishings don't distract from the art, but the raspberry pillows, lampshades, and curtain trim give the room a jazzy Parisian elegance. The furniture is a comfortable mix of traditional upholstery, mid-century-style tables and chairs, and antiques such as the eighteenth-century *bureau plat* on the far wall beneath a painting by 1930s French artist Filipe Cognec. **THIS PAGE:** The painting over the sofa is by Leon Kossoff. All of the double doors throughout the house are painted the same shade of taupe, which creates continuity from room to room and from the inside to the outside. **OPPOSITE PAGE:** The original red leather top on the eighteenth-century *bureau plat* not only stole my heart but also worked beautifully with my blue-and-raspberry scheme. The gilded arm sculpture is from Gray Morell of Los Angeles.

THIS PAGE: Contrasting old-world elements with contemporary forms usually brings out the best in both. The hand-painted wallpaper looks even more sumptuous in the upstairs hallway where I merged it with a wall of graphic horizontal stripes in similar hues. A resin sculpture by Yuriko Yamaguchi is stylishly hung over a bronze bench from Formations, which turns the hall into a gallery. **OPPOSITE PAGE:** To maximize the glamour of the oval powder room, I had the walls covered in silver tea paper. I used silver chains to hang an important Venetian mirror over the contemporary sink that sits on a custom-designed neoclassical base.

You can't see my clients' huge oil painting across from the bed, which inspired me to lacquer the walls a pucey chartreuse, but the complementary colors make this bedroom simultaneously soothing and invigorating. I had a banquette built in the bay window, and it's a lovely spot for morning coffee, as well as a place for the children to hang when they visit the master suite. Uncharacteristically, I did not drape the Dennis & Leen four-poster bed, which gives the room an architectural simplicity, but the custom bedding and damask throws add the requisite dollop of decadent glamour. The wheat-colored herringbone carpet is cozy underfoot, and the antique intaglios over the bed complement the eighteenth-century starburst mirror.

THIS PAGE: I like when there's continuity in a master suite, so the bathroom has the same pucey chartreuse walls as the bedroom. **OPPOSITE PAGE:** There's no denying the glamour of the bathtub sheathed in stainless steel, and I upped the ante by adding my all-time favorite Joel Chen stool that gives any room the requisite pizzazz. For a bit of "Ming bling," I had the Chinese wing chair gilded in 22-karat gold. Pumpkin-colored accents provide contrasting shots of color.

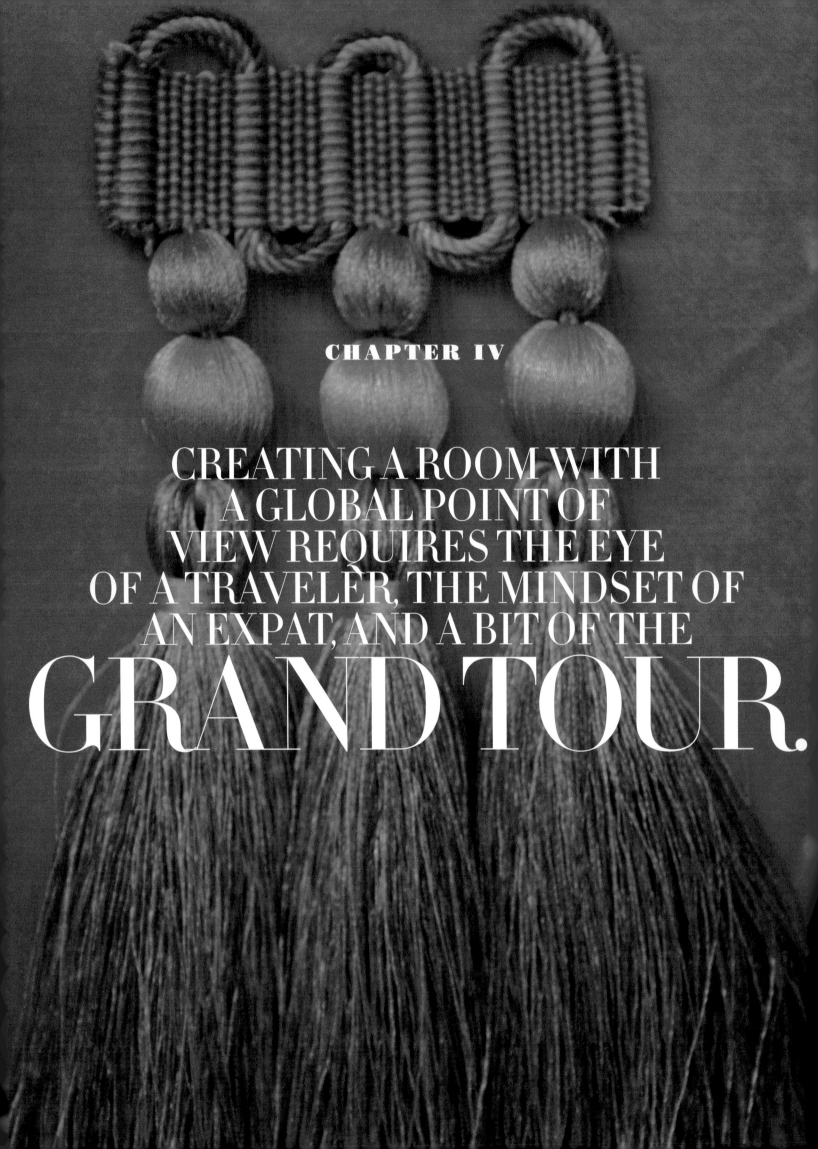

CHAPTER IV

CREATING A ROOM WITH
A GLOBAL POINT OF
VIEW REQUIRES THE EYE
OF A TRAVELER, THE MINDSET OF
AN EXPAT, AND A BIT OF THE
GRAND TOUR.

Indian Miniatures

Paul

...LHALL...

I have an innate wanderlust. Most people I find interesting do. Wherever you travel in the world, there are bazaars, flea markets, and souks with indigenous ceramics, fabrics, carved wood, and metalwork. Invariably, you'll find something that speaks to you—and you should always buy it. As you accumulate things that capture your imagination—whether you're halfway around the world or at a flea market across town—you will no doubt find a common thread that will allow dissimilar objects to live happily together.

The Grand Tour is really a state of mind that taps into my GYPSY soul. You can cultivate it on the Website, 1st dibs, if you wish (which is what I often do!). Of course, I enjoy traveling and collecting in the real world, but when landlocked, 1st Dibs is good for a grand tour fix any day. My version layers *Out of Africa* style with jet-set chic, but the look is actually timeless. For centuries, people have decorated with horns, hides, and archaeological finds that lend a sense of history to a home. It's hard to decide whether the best part of this look is THE HUNT for wonderful things or the freedom to live like a BOHEMIAN in a world where everything and anything seems possible.

It's counterintuitive but this style may be more difficult to get right than any other. You don't actually want your house to look (or smell!) like a third world flea market. You want to fill your house with intriguing, quirky things, but you want the whole to be greater than the sum of its parts. You want harmonic convergence.

PREVIOUS PAGES: California's close ties to the Orient have always influenced my style. Far Eastern pieces—such as the custom-painted bamboo demilune table and antique Chinese vase lamp with its funky shade made from a bamboo wastebasket—are worldly yet all-American. **OPPOSITE PAGE:** A framed piece of Zuber wallpaper in a faux bamboo frame brings a island feel to a house in the heart of Beverly Hills. Chairs slipcovered in a Raoul Textiles print surround an ebonized pedestal game table. The birdcage lends an air of tropical exotica.

The Hunt

When something is irresistible, you should buy it. Pictures, objects, and furnishings that speak to you tend to speak to each other, creating improbably wonderful harmonies.

PREVIOUS PAGES, LEFT: A mesmerizing oversized portrait of a lady sits on a Portuguese table surrounded by Chinese vases and orchids. **RIGHT:** The living room of the historic Buster Keaton estate is warm and worldly, with its mix of continental antiques and Portuguese furniture in a timeless chocolate-and-*crème* setting. **THIS PAGE:** Some of my best finds are family heirlooms that I was smart enough to hold on to. Several friends told me to give away this ebonized Victorian "divan," as my grandmother called it. But once I had it recaned, it went from divan to divine. **OPPOSITE PAGE:** Another attic treasure is the portrait by the esteemed California landscape painter Clyde Scott, whom I never knew but who was a good friend of my grandfather. It's not only sentimental but also amusing—how can you not be intrigued by a man with a cigarette holder?

This bedroom in the old Buster Keaton estate is a tone poem in cream and white with a pleated wall behind the headboard. Though I am known for how I use color, I love the challenge of working with all neutrals and layering whites and ivories in various textures. To me, white is a color. The draperies on the four-poster bed puddle on the floor for a bit of old-world, come-hither glamour. The bedspread is actually a nineteenth-century embroidered silk tablecloth, and a good example of how antique textiles can be used in unexpected ways. The Regency chinoiserie chaise has a cotton faille cushion and a pair of Anglo-Indian mirrors with bone overlay flank the bed.

THIS PAGE: I love giving purpose to unused spaces. I transformed a staircase landing, which opens onto a balcony, into a family sitting room, which brings together themes from the adjacent bedrooms with a boho mix of burlap, cane, rattan, and ebonized English furniture. FOLLOWING PAGES: A patio to me is an outdoor living room, and it should be furnished with as much detail and style as any indoor room. I designed this terrace for a bachelor's pad, so it has a masculine, connoisseur's sensibility. I brought in wooden columns to define the space and hung all-weather curtains from them. The all-weather "wicker" is both handsome and durable. I hung an iron mirror from heavy chains behind the sofa as a backdrop for a tablescape featuring rough stone pots, an antique armillary sphere, a zinc urn, and architectural fragments. My impractical side could not resist adding the bone-inlaid Anglo-Indian chairs, which are only brought outside for parties.

176

THIS PAGE, CLOCKWISE FROM TOP RIGHT: The arched entry from the front hall onto the loggia that runs the entire back span of the casa-style house and has four distinct seating groups; Moroccan carpets complement the restored tile walls; a view from the guest quarters to the loggia; an assortment of painted plates surround a plaster insignia that was original to the house. OPPOSITE PAGE: I played upon the exotic aspects of this tiled wraparound loggia by placing pillows from a multitude of countries on the retro-looking cane furniture that has an old–California glam appeal.

The guest-house living room opens up to the pool on one side and a courtyard on the other. The open stucco arches are hung with Ralph Lauren cotton curtains. To keep it casual and beachy, I upholstered the furniture in a Ralph Lauren stripe. The Chinese teak coffee table adds a traveled and collected note. The elaborate fireplace was cast from an original antique mold from Stonecast Design in Los Angeles and adds old-Hollywood glamour to the mood.

182

THIS PAGE: The washed oak paneling is the star of this Beverly Hills library, and an antique Tansu chest with a raw driftwood finish and an antique Chinese vessel lamp are the ideal supporting players. **OPPOSITE PAGE:** I chose muted neutral tones for the fabrics to complement the paneling. The bookshelves hold exotic vases and baskets from China and South America. I had the reproduction lantern from Mario's Lighting on Fairfax finished to look as if it had always been there, with the same washed-out, patinated wood finish of the entire library. The coffee table is a contemporary foil from Ceylon et Cie, my friend Michelle Nussbaumer's shop. I kept the floors ebonized in here to tie the entire house together, which has ebonized floors throughout.

THIS PAGE: These guest-room twin beds are lighthearted enough to appeal to children but have plenty of chic to seduce adults. The bed's white drapery against the multi-brown raffia wall gives the room an Andalusian spirit. The other walls are white with a brown crown molding that nicely complements the decorative horns and convex mirrors over the beds. **OPPOSITE PAGE:** I had raffia wallpaper mats made for the intaglios that face the twin beds. I placed graphic pillows on vintage rattan McGuire chairs for a modern punch.

It's a universal truth that everyone hangs out in the kitchen, and this house just happens to have a casual, friendly great room adjacent to the kitchen, which I decided should have the ambience of a French souk. Everyone feels at home in this East-meets-West space with its warm red accents that appear in crewel work, ikats, and antique *suzanis*. English upholstered furniture and Federal mirrors lend an air of tradition to the bohemian mix.

THIS PAGE: A multitude of patterns makes a cohesive statement when they relate not only because of color but also because of the texture and character of the fabrics. OPPOSITE PAGE: The breakfast room has an unusual bone-inlay Indian table surrounded by chairs from Pottery Barn that came with the most authentic patina—you'd never know these weren't antique chairs. The garden hats hanging on the bamboo hat rack and the washed linen draperies lend an appropriately informal feel. The raspberry red throw on the table was purchased online from Uzbekistan.

Bohemian

There's a poetry to layering the new and the old with an insouciance that makes it seem as if everything just fell into place.

PREVIOUS PAGES: The new tennis pavilion and guest house at the old Buster Keaton estate was designed to have the same 1920s glamour as the rest of the property. I designed the scalloped facade and pineapple finials that make it amusing like a garden folly, and the scalloped awnings with spear finial poles make it rather recherché.

THIS PAGE: It's not just the sea-grass carpet that makes you want to walk barefoot through this house. The bohemian vibe has been carefully curated: The baskets and birdcage under the nineteenth-century mahogany claw-foot pedestal table topped with not-so-perfectly stacked piles of books create an improvised aura.

OPPOSITE PAGE: Instead of upholstering the ottoman, I draped a zebra-skin throw over it for a more casual, idiosyncratic feel. Slipcovers, mismatched Oriental rugs, and flowing curtains made of cotton ticking are an unexpected foil for refined nineteenth-century Imari plates that hang on the wall.

Draperies and under drapes in multiple patterns have become one of my signatures. For this formal yet unorthodox breakfast room, I mixed pale pink linen, a raspberry Clarence House cotton stripe, and a playful pink ikat that is especially yummy. Everything here has a handmade, cozy quality: the raffia walls, the canvas tablecloth trimmed in a fantastic Ralph Lauren superwide linen fringe that looks like hemp rope, the custom octagonal sea-grass rug that follows the contours of the room. The judicious exoticism comes from a worldly mix that includes Anglo-Indian chairs and Chinese and Italian jester prints, along with papier-mâché English crumbers, which are debonair when hung in a cluster as part of a collection.

The starting point for this guest bedroom was a set of vintage Indian fabric draperies, which I had cut and reworked (by adding some fabric) for bedding and curtains. I decided to really push the bamboo theme—I don't like to do things halfway—which extends from the four-poster bed to the mirrors and the demilunes, which I had painted in a powdery blue. The lampshades were made from bamboo wastebaskets I bought at an Asian import store. I bought twelve at once, and I wish I'd bought more because they are so chic and I've never been able to find them again. The blue rectangle on the wall was not part of the original scheme, but when the room was installed, it seemed too serene so I had a painter come paint color blocks on either side of the bed to add a vibrant jolt. It's important not to feel you've failed if something still seems off after an installation. Decorating is a creative process full of visual surprises when everything finally comes together in three dimensions.

198

THIS PAGE: My penchant for exotic guest rooms is expressed in this Moroccan-themed, tangerine-and-blue room at the hacienda estate in Beverly Hills. The color scheme was inspired by the Oushak rug and the vintage maps that I had framed with royal-blue mats. The lines of the headboard and the mysterious doughnut hole that I dreamed up make a compelling if cryptic statement and so does the fishing net that is layered on top of the edge. I hung antique Chinese saucers over the bed, which is flanked by a pair of Anglo-Indian chests. And what could be more dreamy than custom-made, hand-embroidered sheets from Morocco?

OPPOSITE PAGE: One of my favorite old-world decorating tricks is draping a shawl or throw over a side table. It has a wonderful gypsy feel that can be quite sophisticated when a beautiful bedspread is paired with the right accessories, such as brass Indian lamps and a French mirror. The prosaic paper-bag lampshades complement the window shades made from authentic burlap for an effect that is humble haute style.

Decorating is creating a stage set for people's lives, so I was flattered when fellow L.A. decorator Peter Dunham called this show-house room an "opera." Ralph Lauren generously donated his fabrics, and the ones I chose have an ethnic feel that worked well in this Spanish-style house. I had always wanted to make shell-encrusted pelmets and, finally, this was my opportunity—an eye-catching touch that, along with the wavy lines of the valance and headboard, suggests ocean voyages. I purposely chose vibrant orange walls to balance the old-lady furniture, and the show-house organizers kept asking me to change it. But I knew that they were behaving like nervous clients and I kept putting them off, and we all got a good laugh when this room was chosen for the cover of *House Beautiful*.

203

THIS PAGE: This cover shot for *House Beautiful* shows off detailed fretwork pattern on the luxurious Leontine linens. The Swedish blue-lacquered, faux-ivory, and gilded lamp is one of my most cherished possessions, which is why I am reproducing it for my lighting collection. The painted blue shade adds a contemporary note to an otherwise rather old-fashioned room. One of my favorite tricks for filling empty floor space beneath tables is to use bold oversized vases or other ceramic pieces. **OPPOSITE PAGE:** My milliner's sensibility is evident in the way I use trim, and this double-long fringe from Ralph Lauren is stunning, as are the passementerie rosettes on the sofa's arms. I used multiple fabrics for the upholstery which gives it a couture feel.

Gypsy

The first thing to do when you are ready to decorate is to think of all the things and places that you love.

PREVIOUS PAGES: This stately room needed to be brought to life and no color is as vibrant, fiery, and passionate as red. I envisioned an all-red Andalusian fantasia, but my clients thought that might be overwhelming, so we decided that the walls would be vanilla—but nothing else would. When I don't want a grand room to be too fancy or formal, I rely on my tried-and-true formula: linen fabrics, sea-grass rugs, Indian furniture, and English upholstery, which can be mixed with a wide variety of antiques and artwork. There are several seating areas in this living room, so it functions equally well for intimate gatherings and large parties. **THIS PAGE:** The tassel trim on the matching sofas makes me think of flamenco dancers. The turned bench is based on my mother's childhood piano bench and it's such a perfect piece that I regularly reproduce it for clients. I've slipcovered it in a fabulous Gastón y Daniela stripe. **OPPOSITE PAGE:** A perky ranunculus in a silver compote begins to shed petals on a painted Chinese box.

THIS PAGE, CLOCKWISE FROM TOP LEFT: Decadence is in the details: Moroccan-flavored nailheads on the apron of a slipper chair; a nineteenth-century bookcase with intricately inlaid ivory patterning; a collection of antique red-leather classics that reflect my obsessiveness when it comes to pushing a theme; a gilded Italian baluster lamp sheds light on vintage Murano birds that have the same profile as the flamingos in the watercolor that I commissioned from artist Aija Gibson, whom I asked to make it look like an old Indian Tree of Life panel. **OPPOSITE PAGE:** By layering a *suzani* on a chaise and pairing it with a Syrian game table and Indian armchair, I made this corner of the living room seem like a super-stylish souk.

PREVIOUS PAGES, LEFT: An English mother-of-pearl tray, a gilded candlestick, and a Chinese bowl sit on an intricately carved Moroccan table, which is bohemian at its most refined. **RIGHT:** The *suzani* on the sofa provides a genuine exotic flavor—it came straight from Uzbekistan and still had the funky smell of the marketplace for a while. Not everybody can put up with that, but I don't mind because exploration is in my blood: I am a descendant of Sir Walter Raleigh, and I'm not sure whether that's a blessing or a curse. **OPPOSITE PAGE:** I could not have dreamed up a better silhouette for the doorway to the dining room, which is original to the 1922 hacienda estate. I had the floors and walls ebonized for an austere, modern take on tradition. The entrance is flanked by two shiny brass Indian wastebaskets that I repurposed as jardinieres. **THIS PAGE:** To glitz up the Spanish colonial sideboard, I paired a gilded sunburst mirror with overscaled, blue-and-white Chinese lamps whose bases I had finished in 22-karat gold to create a bit of a sensation. **FOLLOWING PAGES:** The oceanic dining room of the Hacienda estate has blue grasscloth walls and Anglo-Indian Regency-style chairs. The iron lantern was aged so it looked original to the 1920s house. The palms give the room a Casablanca vibe. The console table is covered in burlap with passementerie frogs that I designed.

CHAPTER V

DESIGN IS LIKE

THEATER.

THE BETTER THE SETS, THE
BETTER THE PLAY.
AS IN LIFE, IF THE PLAY ISN'T
GOOD, YOU MIGHT
AS WELL LIKE THE SET.

I'm a drama queen. I like rooms that resonate wit and self-assurance and unapologetically say, *This is who I am—take it or leave it!* Theatrical rooms are very particular; they are undeniably fabulous. Sometimes, they have a zanily obsessive quality, a quirky, one-of-a-kindness. But even when they have an exuberant spirit, they must be poised and polished, too.

A theatrical room can be CLASSIC or outrageous. It ought to be welcoming, gracious and drop-dead gorgeous—so stunning that you are rendered speechless. It can be modern and bold, a GRAPHIC statement with contrasting colors, fabrics, and materials. Or it can be a dizzy explosion of EXOTIC elements that causes a sense of wonder and delight.

There is no formula for this type of decorating. It's as individual as the clients, a reflection of their aspirations. Yet form must follow function to create backdrops where you can fully enjoy the sensual pleasures of everyday life. What can be more energizing than to feel a thrill every time you enter your library or bedroom? What can be more satisfying than to know your house guests feel at ease in your home? What is more important than the sense of comfort you feel every time you enter through the front door? If you indulge your magnificent OBSESSIONS then your home will be a reflection of your heart.

PREVIOUS PAGES, LEFT: A gilded Regency-style chair in black patent leather. RIGHT: View of the Vein living room from the hallway showcasing the original fluted curved entry walls, accentuating the grandeur of days gone by. OPPOSITE PAGE: I designed the living room of the Vein residence with two mirror-image seating groups to maximize the space while creating a central walkway so that there would be good flow for large cocktail parties. I love the contrast of the simple, custom-made L-shaped sofa upholstered in a *crème* cotton velvet with the brawny gilded French chair, classic Jansen coffee table, and the very feminine *doré gueridon* side table. The painting always makes me laugh, because it sums up how I sometimes feel.

Living rooms are meant for entertaining. They must function beautifully for large soirees and intimate dinner parties.

Classic

OPPOSITE PAGE: I love passementerie details such as the Greek key trim and the opulent rosette and tassel that enliven an otherwise staid sofa. **THIS PAGE:** An antique Regency window-high console with dramatic lion column legs is flanked by two armchairs. The nineteenth-century Louis XVI fauteuil in the foreground is upholstered in black leather fabric with a bright yellow Clarence House silk bolster that expands upon the Greek key motif.
FOLLOWING PAGES: The walls were originally *crème*, and it was way too sober for my taste so I begged my clients to paint the walls a charcoal gray, which I think is the ultimate neutral. As I knew it would, the gray walls made every other element in the room pop. I came up with this unorthodox floor plan that is anchored by a large-scale, low-backed pouf that would not only relate to all three conversation groups but also make this room, full of furniture, seem airy and like three contiguous salons. The over-scaled nineteenth-century French mirror lends a sense of grandeur that is balanced by the zesty yellow-and-black curtains hung on silver-plated French hardware rods close to the ceiling (instead of the window frame), which contributes to the epic feel of the room.

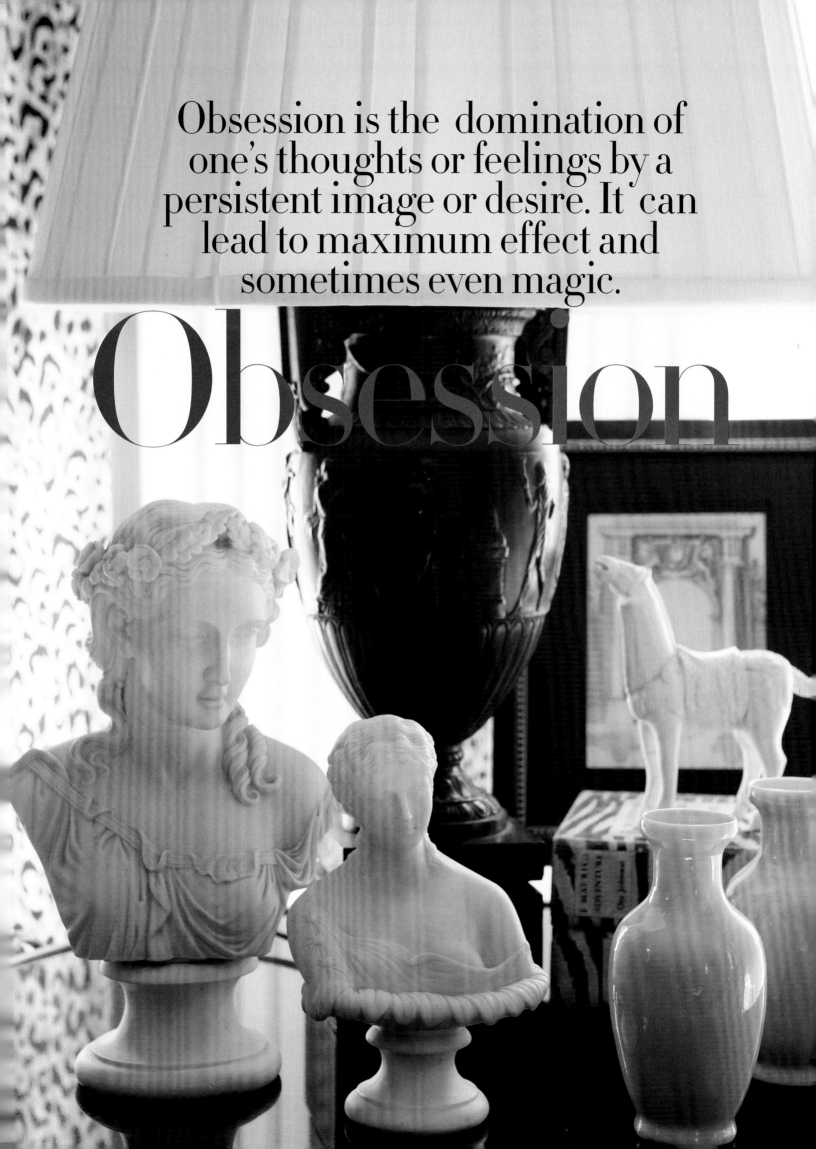

Obsession is the domination of one's thoughts or feelings by a persistent image or desire. It can lead to maximum effect and sometimes even magic.

Obsession

PREVIOUS PAGES: My all-leopard-print library is a bit over-the-top, but it is the perfect lair for me. A carved bone horse stands on a copy of *I Married Adventure*, a vintage book that people collect because of its zebra-striped cover. THIS PAGE: This is the sunniest side of the sunroom. I didn't invent the head-to-toe animal-print room but I think I've made the concept my own without making it look like a bordello by giving it a girly, French feel with pieces such as the black-and-gold Directoire chandelier. OPPOSITE PAGE: This wall-scape design is what we in my office call "premeditated whimsy," which is a calculated way of making a bunch of mismatched stuff go together. Here, the unifying theme is the frames that are black, gold, or a combination of the two. Before I hang wall-scapes, I lay them on the floor so I can fill in the bald spots and create balance. I had planned to add a few more pieces to the wall, but I never did, so this is still really a work in progress. FOLLOWING PAGES: When you see the full expanse of the sunroom, you see how the uniform leopard-print-fabric walls, curtains, and upholstery create a space that is more comforting than zany. The boldly striped chairs, shades, and pillows make the leopard print seem almost subdued, and of course the room gets its raison d'être because it's flooded with light.

Graphic

Modernism isn't a period or
a style; it's an attitude.

PREVIOUS PAGES: A red patent-leather pillow against a graphic pillow made of David Hicks fabric is the apotheosis of mod. The high-contrast scheme is echoed by the juxtaposition of a black Kartell Bourgie lamp, contemporary mercury glass, and Han-inspired ceramic soldiers. THIS PAGE: This Pop Art–inspired room has a simple layout that is focused on the fireplace and flat-screen TV over it on the right side of the room. Though the upholstery is cozy and quiet, the Madeline Weinrib rug provides a lot of punch, along with the bold, horizontally color-blocked canvas curtains. I had the insides of the bookshelves painted black, which makes the books and white objets d'art seem especially graphic.

THIS PAGE: Giving antiques a new complexion by placing them in modern settings always excites me. In the redecorated Kings Road guest house, the royal-navy-blue-and-white scheme extends to the antique walls, chairs, and the custom stenciled sea-grass rug. The gessoed wood sconces and pier mirror are antiques, but the rope vanity is pure 1950s Hollywood. The nineteenth-century French boudoir chair is upholstered in blue velvet.

OPPOSITE PAGE: I used pink for punctuation marks in this room. I had the ceiling of the bed painted pink, which casts a rosy glow. The stools in front of the bed came from the flea market and I loved the old-world quality of the tufted tops, so I had them reupholstered in the same blue velvet. I kept the castors, too, because I imagined someone pulling one up to the bed as a place to pile magazines.

Remember when this room was gray and white? (See page 24.) It was so soigné and utterly me. But when I turned it into a guest room I took everything that was gray and redesigned it all in royal-navy blue while keeping everything white just as it was. The transformation was not limited to the color scheme. I had a big velvet ottoman made with gilded antique metal cast legs that I removed from a worn-out coffee table I had bought at auction because the legs were so fantastic. The soft pink pillows and the pink artwork by Mia Moretti over the fireplace keep the room from being overzealous. Ultimately, the rug is what gives the room its va va voom.

240

THIS PAGE: I like to have fun with guest rooms, and the editors at the sadly defunct *Domino* magazine loved this room. It's my contemporary spin on chinoiserie, the eighteenth-century European take on Chinese art and style, which has been especially popular on the West Coast for decades. I've made it modern with the graphic wall treatment and whimsical pagoda headboard that makes guests feel like they're on a good-humored adventure.
OPPOSITE PAGE: When confronted with a room that has little natural light, I don't fight it. I go with it—and make it a little jewel. For this rather dark library, I made cocoa brown the dominant color and then spiced it up with a graphic white border and a ruby-red ceiling; the red is taken from a David Hockney painting on the right wall. The room sparkles because of the brass Maison Jansen coffee tables and gilded bookshelves, and it's lighthearted, too, because of the curtains made from a bold chinoiserie toile by Quadrille.

THIS PAGE AND OPPOSITE PAGE: Yellow is such a brilliant color—the color of daffodils, lemons, and *National Geographic* magazines—and yet it can be difficult to use. For a bachelor's TV room, I painted the walls black and then used yellow and white to create a space that is both rugged and cheery, sleek but comfy. Stripes are the leitmotif, which I associate with racing and sports cars, and men! Vintage pool balls in a basket are eye candy on the ottoman, adding a playful note to the room, and the zebra-skin rug signifies that this is a manly den.

This loggia is a stage meant to be filled with people—an outdoor space designed for entertaining that made me think of the "Ascot Gavotte" scene in *My Fair Lady*. I chose big cabana stripes for the curtains and cushions, but it's the striped walls that make this scenario so dramatic. Without the striped walls, it would have no dazzle and we all need some dazzle in our lives. The overscaled black-lacquered planters and urns on pedestals add an English country-house element to this intrinsically elegant Tudor house in Hancock Park.

246

Some clients have more gumption than others, and this room started out ten years ago as a nursery for twin girls with cribs that had Mondrian-inspired crib skirts and bumpers. It was certainly a cutting-edge children's room at the time and it has transitioned quite well. As they got older, I designed new twin beds with shimmering nickel-plated finials that match those on the valences. The opposite side of the lemon-yellow room has floor-to-ceiling shelves where the girls store their toys in baskets. The rug is contemporary Chinese.

248

OPPOSITE PAGE: I admit that I was slightly nervous when I was hired to decorate my first hotel, the Luxe on Sunset Boulevard in Bel Air, which was a 1980s pink granite number that needed to be updated. There are different standards for fabrics and furniture when you are designing a hotel that will be filled with people around the clock, so I hired a staff well versed in hotel technicalities to assist me. More modern and masculine than most of my published work, the hotel's lobby feels residential because of elements such as the homey, nine-foot–tall studded leather screen, the tiered–linen lighting fixture that I designed instead of the usual chandelier, and the giant shell photographs I commissioned. **THIS PAGE:** The seating area near the concierge seems like a sophisticated guy's home, with its modern wing chairs and bookshelves filled with Asian antiques.

The Neapolitan-ice-cream
color theme of the bar
may be apparent only to
me, but I think it sets the
ideal mood for cocktails.
I used the existing soffits
to define the seating areas
with custom chocolate-
colored linen velvet settees,
and I added creamy pillows
as accents. The taupe raffia
walls mimic the limestone
floors throughout the
hotel; the bar's custom
chocolate-and-cream rug is
so popular it is now part of
Shaw Carpets' hospitality
line. I commissioned
the ice-cream-inspired
paintings by Mia Moretti,
because I couldn't find
anything that had exactly
the right amount of pink I
envisioned for the walls.

252

Inspiration is often serendipitous. For this redo of the Kings Road guesthouse media room, the starting point was a 1950s Mark Shaw fashion photo and a vintage-looking chintz with blowsy peonies on a black ground. Every color stripe on the wall can be found on that chintz pillow. Working with my painter, we came up with a random pattern of colorful stripes; it felt like we were collaborating on a fun art project. The wall is so powerful that I thought anything but white furniture might be de trop.

THIS PAGE, TOP: At the Luxe Hotel, I was able to design suites that have many of the elements of guest rooms I've designed for myself and my clients. The bed has elaborate draperies made of red-and-brown cotton canvas, and I placed two elm Chinese throne chairs in front of it. Across from the bed, I placed rush daybeds instead of the typical sofas. **BOTTOM:** Color-block curtains are a leitmotif in this hotel, and I love how we got the stripe on the wall and the curtains to line up in this blue and brown suite, where I used a Chinese garden stool as an end table, as I do at home. **OPPOSITE PAGE:** A simple red, white, and brown color scheme with pale wood furniture has a universal appeal that is especially well suited to a hotel that wants to make people from around the world feel at home.

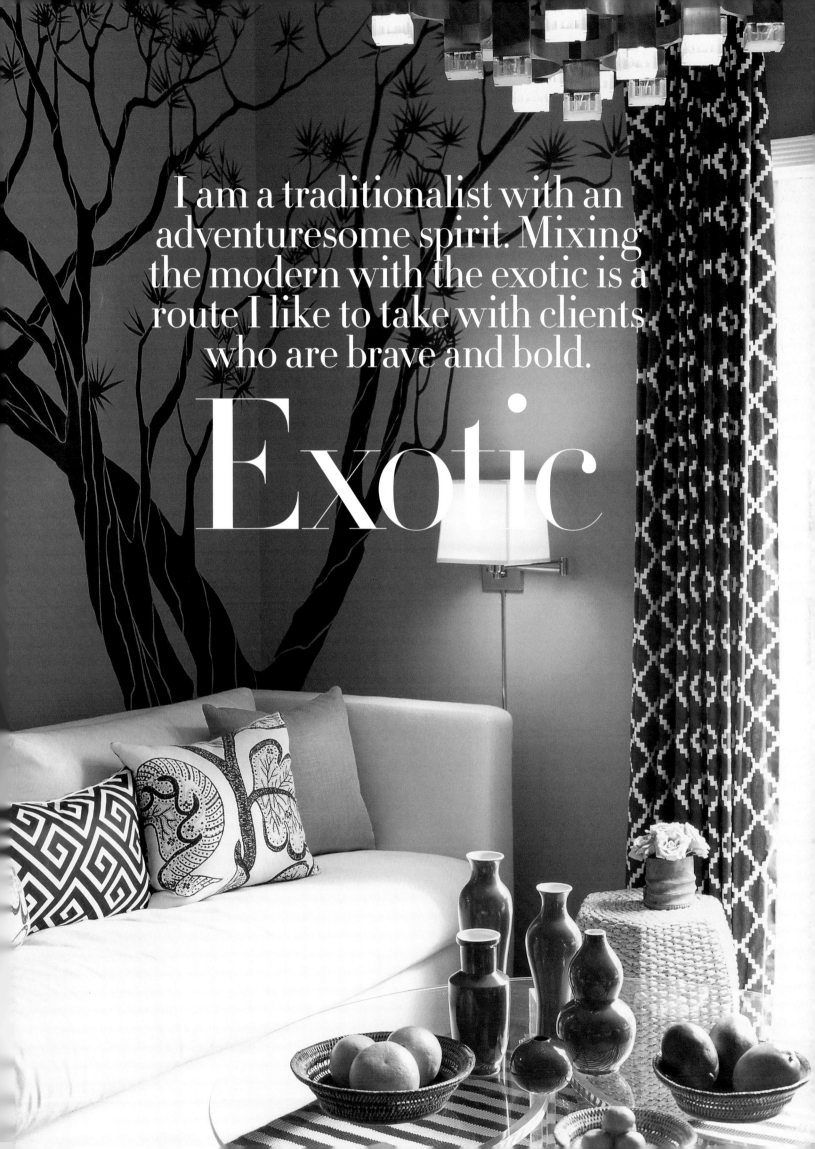

I am a traditionalist with an adventuresome spirit. Mixing the modern with the exotic is a route I like to take with clients who are brave and bold.

Exotic

By keeping the color scheme simple—tangerine, brown, and white—I could bring in lots of tribal-inspired patterns and still maintain the room's equilibrium for this client's sunroom. On the wall, I had artist Jefferson Miles paint a graphic Asian-inspired tree that gives the room a modern and gutsy sensibility. **THIS PAGE:** Breakfast rooms are a great place to be whimsical. I like to set an example for my clients by showing them how they can collect almost anything. In this Beverly Hills kitchen, I put together an amusing collection of Hawaiian fish bowls and fish molds that was as much fun to hunt for as to figure out how to display. I love how they look like they're all swimming in the same direction on the striped walls that were inspired by surfers' board shorts. **OPPOSITE PAGE:** In another Beverly Hills kitchen, I put together an assortment of gilded starburst mirrors, metal stars, and convex mirrors that would give the clients flexibility if they wanted to add to the collection. It was a lighthearted way to add light to a dark corner. A built-in banquette is where the children have snacks.

OPPOSITE PAGE: I am one of the few decorators I know who admit to not envisioning everything in advance. When we finished this dining room, which features a zebra-hide-trimmed mirror and a circle-in-a-square rug by Denis Colomb, I realized that the entry hall lacked definition, so I had a brown graphic trim painted to follow the moldings and baseboards and it made all the difference in the world. **THIS PAGE:** A vintage zebra-skin bench beneath a console with an eye-popping shell collection and modern tortoiseshell lamps reflect a worldly sensibility.

My clients, the Salkes,
had a good collection
of modern art as well
as Knoll, Le Corbusier,
and Mies van der Rohe
furniture, which was the
starting point for this
living room. I did not
want to do too much
(which is not really my
normal modus operandi),
because I wanted to
focus on the simplicity of
the furnishings. Instead
of a traditional seating
group, I used a pair of
Pucci chaises with a
multipurpose ottoman.
The custom rug with the
square centering the room
maintains the graphic
leitmotif of this house.
FOLLOWING PAGES: Until
we could find the right
artwork to hang in the
living room, I had circles
painted on the chocolate-
brown walls above the
matching banquettes.
I love how they look,
especially when you
take in the circle-in-the-
square rug in the dining
room beyond.

264

ACCESSORIES AND CURIOSITIES

Deyrolle
46 Rue du Bac
75007 Paris, France
Tel: 01 4222 3007
www.deyrolle.com

John Derian Company
6 East Second Street
New York, NY 10003
Tel: 212.677.3917
Fax: 212.677.7197
E-mail: shop@johnderian.com
http://johnderian.com

BATH FIXTURES

Lefroy Brooks
Ibroc House
Essex Road
Hoddesdon, Hertfordshire
EN11 0QS
United Kingdom
Tel: 19 9270 8316
Fax: 19 9270 8317
www.lefroybrooks.com

Water Works
60 Backus Avenue
Danbury, CT 06810
Tel: 800-899-6757
www.waterworks.com

BOOKSTORES, ART AND DESIGN

Archivia Books
993 Lexington Avenue
New York, NY 10021
Tel: 212-570-9565
Fax: 212-570-9561
E-mail: info@archiviabooks.com
www.archiviabooks.com

CUSTOM ANTIQUE MIRRORS

Campbell Glass Shop
6234 South Gramercy Place
Los Angeles, CA 90047-1305
Tel: 323-735-1445
www.campbellglass.com

CUSTOM PAINTED FLOORS AND COLOR CONSULTING

Scott Flax Studio
1660 Stanford Street
Santa Monica, CA 90404
Tel: 310-829-1445
Fax: 310-829-9484
E-mail: scottflax@aol.com.
www.scottflax.com

DECORATIVE CHINOISERIE AND PAINTING

Maria Apelo Cruz
Tel: 818-921-0530
E-mail: maria@apelocruz.com
http://apelocruz.com

EMBROIDERY—CUSTOM

Villa Savoia, Inc.
E-mail: Michael@villasavoiainc.com
www.villasavoia.net

FURNITURE—ANTIQUE, VINTAGE, AND REPRODUCTION

Amy Perlin Antiques
306 E. 61st Street
New York, NY 10021
Tel: 212-593-5756
Fax 212-593-5240
www.amyperlinantiques.com

Asli Tunca
Nuru Ziya Sok. No 34/20
Galatasaray 34433
Istanbul, Turkey
Tel: 21 2251 7057
Fax: 21 2245 4703
E-mail: info@aslitunca.com
www.aslitunca.com

Blackman Cruz
836 North Highland Avenue
Los Angeles, CA 90038
Tel: 323-466-8600
www.blackmancruz.com

Ceylon et Cie
1319 Dragon Street
Dallas, TX 75207
Tel: 214 742 7632
Fax: 214-742-7631
E-mail: ceylonetcie@sbcglobal.net
www.ceylonetcie.com

Duane Modern
176 Duane Street
New York, NY 10013
Tel: 212-625-8066
Fax: 212-625-8065
E-mail: info@duanemodern.com
www.duanemodern.com

1st Dibs
http://1stdibs.com

Hollyhock
927 N. La Cienega Boulevard
Los Angeles, CA 90069
www.hollyhockinc.com

Ingeborg Ravestijn Antiques
Oudenlandsdijkje 9
1141 PH Monnikendam
The Netherlands (outside Amsterdam)
Tel: 31 20 625 7720
www.ravestijn-antiques.nl

JED
27 Washington Street
Sag Harbor, NY 11963-4437
Tel: 631-725-6411

J.F. Chen
941 North Highland Avenue
Los Angeles, CA 90038
Tel: 323-466-9700
Fax: 323-469-1600
E-Mail: gabrielle@jfchen.com

John Rosselli
Antiques & Decorations
306 East 61st Street_Ground Floor
New York, NY 10065
Tel: 212-750-0060
Fax: 212-750-0076
Mari Ann Maher
E-mail: info@johnrosselli.com
www.johnroselliantiques.com

Lars Bolander
72 Gansevoort Street
New York, NY 10014
Tel: 212-924-1000
Fax: 212-229-2375
www.larsbolander.com

Lief
646 North Almont Drive
West Hollywood, CA 90069
Tel: 310-492-0033
Fax: 310-492-0026
E-mail: info@liefalmont.com
www.liefalmont.com

Marché Paul-Bert
Paris Saint-Ouen Flea Market
18 Rue Paul Bert
93400 Saint-Ouen, France

Nicholas Haslam, Ltd.
12-14 Holbein Place
London SW1W 8NL
United Kingdom
Tel: 020 7730 8623
www.nicholashaslam.com

Oscar & Clothilde
Styrmansgatan 10-12
114 54 Stockholm, Sweden
Tel: 08 611 5300
Fax: 08 611 5332
E-mail: oscar@oscarclothilde.com
www.oscarclothilde.com

Paul Marra Design
868 N La Cienega Boulevard
Los Angeles, CA 90069
Tel: 310-659-8190
Fax: 310-659-8107
E-mail: paulmarradesign@sbcglobal.net
www.paulmarradesign.com

Richard Shapiro
8905 Melrose Avenue
Los Angeles, CA 90069
Tel: 310-275-6700
Fax: 310-275-6723
www.studiolo.com

Stéphane Olivier
La Petite Maison
10 Rue Paul Bert
93400 St-Ouen, France
Tel: 33 1 4010 5669
Fax: 33 1 4012 2771
E-mail: webinfo@stephaneolivier.fr
www.stephaneolivier.fr

Todd Alexander Romano
232 East 59th Street, 4th Floor
New York, New York 10022
Tel: 212-421-7722
E-mail: info@toddromanohome.com
www.toddromanohome.com

FABRIC AND WALLPAPER

Clarence House
979 Third Avenue
New York, NY 10022-1295
(212) 752-2890
www.clarencehouse.com

Colefax and Fowler
39 Brook Street
London W1K 4JE
United Kingdom
Tel: 20 7493 2231
Fax: 20 7373 7916
www.colefax.com

Cowtan and Tout
111 Eighth Avenue, Suite 930
New York, NY 10011
Tel: 212-647-6900
Fax: 212-647-6906
www.cowtan.com

F Schumacher & Co
8687 Melrose Avenue,
Suite B-489
Los Angeles, CA 90069-7108
Tel: 310-652-5353
Fax: 310-652-5803
www.fschumacher.com

Hollywood at Home
724 N. La Cienega Boulevard
Los Angeles, CA 90069
Tel: 310-273-6200
Fax: 310-273-1438
E-mail: info@
hollywoodathome.com
www.hollywoodathome.com

Madeline Weinrib Atelier
ABC Carpet & Home
888 Broadway, the 6th floor
New York, NY 10003
212.473.3000 x3780
E-mail: contact@
madelineweinrib.com
www.madelineweinrib.com

Scalamandré Silks
222 East 59th Street
New York, NY 10022
Tel: 212-980-3888

**WALLPAPER—
HANDPAINTED**

De Gournay
210 Fifth Avenue, 8th Floor
New York, NY 10010
Tel: 212 564 9750
Fax: 212-564-9067
www.degournay.com

Paul Montgomery Studio
P.O. Box 976
Churchville, VA 24421
Tel: 540-337-6600
Fax: 540-337-6966
E-mail: info@
paulmontgomery.com
www.paulmontgomery.com

HARDWARE—
EUROPEAN-STYLE

The Golden Lion
225 North Robertson
Boulevard
Beverly Hills, CA 90211
Tel: 310-246-1752
Fax: 310-246-1691
E-mail: info@thegoldenlion.
com
www.thegoldenlion.com

Van Dyke's Restorers
Tel: 800-237-8833
www.vandykes.com

LIGHTING

Ann Morris
239 East 60th Street
New York, NY 10022
Tel: 212-755-3308

Christopher Spitzmiller, Inc.
248 W. 35th Street
New York, NY 10018
Tel: 212-563-1144
Fax: 212-563-4144
E-mail: info@
christopherspitzmiller.com
www.christopherspitzmiller.
com

Paul Ferrante
8464 Melrose Place
Los Angeles, CA 90069
Tel: 323-653-4142
Fax: 323-653-6504
www.paulferrante.com

Robert Abbey, Inc.
Tel: 866-203-5392
Fax: 815-366-0385
www.robertabbey.com

LINENS

Boutique D. Porthault
470 Park Avenue
New York, NY 10022
Tel: 212-688-1660
E-mail: newyork@
dporthaultparis.com
http://dporthault.com

Frette
459 N. Rodeo Drive
Beverly Hills, CA 90210
Tel: 310-273-8540
www.frette.com

Leontine Linens
Tel: 800-876-4799
www.leontinelinens.com

Matouk
http://matouk.com

Pratesi
9024 Burton Way
Beverly Hills, CA 90211
Tel: 310-274-7661
www.pratesi.com

**METAL PLATING AND
METALWORK**

**Beverly Hills Plating
Works**
243 N Robertson Boulevard
Beverly Hills, CA 90211-1703
Tel: 310-271-1701

**CUSTOM ARTISANAL
METALWORK**

Juan Carlos Pallarols |
Maestro Orfebre
Defensa 1039
Buenos Aires, Argentina
Tel: 11 4300 6555
www.pallarols.com.ar
E-mail: info@pallarols.com.ar

**OUTDOOR, GARDEN,
AND ACCESSORIES**

Inner Gardens
8925 Melrose Avenue
West Hollywood, CA 90069
Phone: 310-492-9990
Fax: 310-492-9992
ww.innergardens.com

JANUS et Cie
8687 Melrose Avenue,
Suite B193
West Hollywood, CA 90069
Tel: 310-652-7090
Fax: 310-652-1284
www.janusetcie.com

Mecox Gardens
www.mecoxgardens.com

Treillage, Ltd.
1015 Lexington Ave.
New York, NY 10021
Tel: 212-988-8800
Fax: 212-988-8810
www.treillageonline.com

PACKING AND SHIPPING

Hedley's Humpers
3 St. Leonard's Road
London
NMW10 6F5
United Kingdom
Tel: 018 1965 8733
www.hedleyshumpers.com

Plycon Van Lines
4240 W. 190th Street, Suite C
Torrance, CA 90504
Tel: 310-419-1200
Fax: 310-419-6110
www.plycongroup.com

PAINT

Farrow & Ball
Tel: 888 511 1121
www.farrow-ball.com

Fine Paints of Europe
Tel: 800-332-1556
E-mail: info@finepaints.com
www.finepaintsofeurope.com

PASSEMENTERIE TRIM

Houles
Houles USA, Inc
979 Third Ave, Suite 1200
New York, NY 10022
Tel: 212-935-3900
Fax: 212-838-5611
www.houles.com

Samuel & Sons
983 Third Avenue
New York, NY 10022
Tel: 212-704-8000
Fax: 212-704-8044
E-mail: info@samuelandsons.
com
www.samuelandsons.com

RUGS

AM Collections
584 Broadway, Suite 201
New York, New York 10012
Tel: 212-625-2616
Fax: 212-625-2617
www.amcollections.com

Patterson, Flynn & Martin
www.patttersonflynnmartin

Stark Carpet
www.starkcarpet.com

STONE AND TILE

Ann Sacks
8935 Beverly Boulevard
Los Angeles, CA 90048
Tel: 310-273-0700
Fax: 310-273-0800
www.annsacks.com

Exquisite Surfaces
www.xsurfaces.com

ACKNOWLEDGMENTS

To my super-talented book team without whom I would not have a book, nor known how to navigate the waters of publishing or complexities of book design. To my book agent, Jill Cohen, who has encouraged me in every way possible and spent countless hours reviewing more than she had to with endless discussions on much more than books: thank you for being all that and a friend. To the magnificently talented Doug Turshen, whose work has been an inspiration to me ever since I opened a Caroline Roehm book, long before I knew books had book designers. Thank you for making a dream come true. I look forward to more. A great thanks to the magician Dan Shaw for making eloquent sense out of pages of babble while still retaining my unique sense of humor. To the debonair Charles Miers of Rizzoli who has let me express myself without question: double foil says it all. You spoiled me and I loved it. Thank you. To the astute Kathleen Jayes, for your attention to image and detail and your easygoing manner, without which nothing would run smoothly…oh yes, and the patience with title changes. You are a saint.

To my branding agent Keith Granet, also a "Family Feud" alumnus (yes, it's true), for believing in me and pointing me in the right direction while encouraging me to be me, because after all everyone else is taken. Thank you.

To my great licensees Robert Abbey Inc, specifically Darlene Salatto Rose, Ken Wilkinson, and dear Jeffrey Rose, now at peace, thank you for trying something new and believing in my talent.

To my family whose support has allowed me since youth to discover and nurture my creative talents. First and foremost to the memory of my mother, who encouraged me to believe in following my inspiration. Without her love I would never have had the courage to put myself out there. You have my eternal love and gratitude. I wish you were here to share this. To my brothers, Desmond Bonaventure and John James Gilbert, for holding down the fort of family business matters and freeing your sister up to pursue her dreams, as well as their wives, Lori and Julie, and my three nieces, Tara, Jenae, and Claire Jean. To my impeccable father for showing me what it means to be British. To my dear Aunt Phyllis and Uncle Bruce for every picture perfect holiday from Christmas to Easter that any child would envy and which now inspire my entertaining. I will cherish the memory of those beautiful table settings, extensive craft projects, and holiday warmth for the rest of my life. Last of all, to my adorable godchildren Gigi Bren, Oliver Bren, Anais Nussbaumer, Fig Camille Abner, and honorable godchildren Anias Abner and Francesca Forge, for reminding me how magically inspiring youth is.

To my dearest John who has loved all versions of me most of my adult life. My deepest love and gratitude for your unconditional love and acceptance of my truest self without whom this endeavor would not be complete.

A special thanks to the following clients and collaborators who trusted me and my vision while often becoming friends: Kendra and Efrem Harkham, Luxe Hotel Bel Air, Jill And Mark Freeman, Eden and Steven Romick, Marisa Tomei , Ed and Mindy Mann, Jennifer and Bert Salke, Beverly Hills Properties, The Seaton Company, Barry Perlman, The Bedrossian Family, Shari and Ed Glazer, Kimm and Al Uzielli, Thais Bren and Fred Couples, Renee Zelwegger, The City of Beverly Hills, Ryan Murphy, Jason Shaw, Jon and Ellen Vein, The Gotham Group, John Bercsi Development, Greystone Mansion, The Veranda Greystone Showhouse, House Beautiful Brentwood and Bel Air Showhouses, Mr. and Mrs. Robert Tebbe, The Gilbert Family, Pamela Brooks, and Mr. and Mrs. Miller.

All my friends and supporters throughout the years who have always encouraged every creative endeavor and then some: my dearest friend and fashion playmate Danielle King; my surrogate sister Michelle Nussbaumer, her husband, Bernard, and their children Nile, Anais, Axel and Andreas for contributing to a life of design by seeing the world together with great aplomb; Jill Nicholson for years of patient listening; Dory and Marsh Forge and your beautiful daughters for "getting in"; Eric Hughes my design sounding board; John Carrabino for telling me I am above it; Nathan Turner, my accidental personal chef; Jennifer Nicholson, Carrie Doyle, Sam Storkerson, Stacie Stukin, Claudia Benvenuto, Kim Alexandriuk, Molly Isaksen, The Bercsi Family, Ted Russell and Matthew Rolston, Charles Russell, dazzling Lulu Powers and Steve Danelian, the ever charming Tony Williams, Ruth and Todd Black; the talented Richard Sherman who has inspired me for 25 years; Jack "Mr. Lady" Deamer; Joel and Margaret Chen; the galvanizing Julie Hunter; Gregory Parkinson for looking like Halston; Leslie Rubinoff; talented and witty Bridget Gless and chivalrous Paul Keller; Milly de Cabrol and Jeffrey Podolsky, who always make me laugh; Konstantine Kakanias, for the constant inspiration to live life to the fullest you carry with you, and of course, my beautiful coveted drawings. Last but not least to my very special friend Miguel Flores-Vianna who has urged me to move forward and trust my vision with constant support since the day we met: thank you for your friendship, endless photography, and constantly inspiring presence and style.

To the following magazine editors who have published my work over the years: Dominique Browning, Dara Caponigro, Stephen Drucker, Carolyn Englefield, Pamela Fiore, Jennifer Smith Hale, John Huey, Pamela Lerner Jaccarino, Barbara King, Martha McCully, Marian McEvoy, Mary Kate Mcgrath, Mark Mayfield, Sarah Medford, Alexandria Abramian Mott, Anna Murphy, Deborah Needleman, Lisa Newsom, Degen Pener, Elfreda Pownall, Margaret Russell, Doretta Sperduto, Andrea Stanford, Newell Turner, Sari Tuschman, Michael Wollaeger, and Zeng Xiangmin. A special thanks as well to the positive and supportive blogger Ronda Carman.

There are no projects that make it to completion without the help of multiple people and their respective dedication, hard work, and often unrecognized talents. Without the support of the following staff, associates, and posse, past and present, there would be no book—nor anything completed for that matter. To my special little Addams Family, James Burkhammer III and Heather Ashton, thank you for years of support and lots good laughs at MMI. To my dear Julia Sucher and your talented sister, Mia Moretti, for both always being inventive and ready to go with smiles on your faces. To super streamlined Nancy Isaacs, whom I can always trust to get the job done, as well as bubbly Mia Elfassy, efficient Kim Ferguson who loves a good credit, stylish Lavin Marez, super organized Erica Rood, Tracy Hudak, Kelly Evans for whom the list is endless, Victoria Romeyn, Jamie Covington, creative Rudy Estrada, Robert Catalan, Troy and Wip, Will Kingman, and Natasha Zarchas—all of whom I am grateful to for sharing my desire to get the job done.

To my photographers who immortalize what designers do, capturing rooms at their best. A very special thanks to both Melanie Acevedo and Victoria Pearson for understanding what is special about my work and taking the extra time to give it all the schzooschze factor it deserves! A grateful thanks to Tom Casey, John Coolidge, Grey Crawford, Karyn Millet, Jean Randazzo, Jessica Shokrian, Tim Street Porter, Robert Trachtenberg, Simon Upton, Miguel Flores-Vianna, Coral Von Zumwalt, and Dominique Vorillon for their invaluable contribution to this book.

PHOTOGRAPHY AND ILLUSTRATION CREDITS

Melanie Acevedo: pages 2, 3, 11, 13, 14, 15, 16, 17, 18, 19, 20, 21, 22, 23, 24, 25, 26, 27, 28, 29, 30, 31, 32, 33, 44, 45, 46, 47, 49 (top left and top right), 50, 51, 52, 53, 67, 69, 70, 71, 72, 73, 90, 91, 115, 122, 123, 125, 126 (top left and top right), 127, 170, 171, 172, 173, 174, 175, 229, 230, 231, 232, 233

Tom Casey: pages 117, 228, 250, 251, 252, 253

John Coolidge: page 96 (top right, bottom left)

Grey Crawford: pages 202, 203, 204, 256 (both images), 257

Konstantine Kakanias: page 7

Mary Mcdonald: pages 5, 10, 34, 60, 74, 114, 166, 220

Victoria Pearson: pages 61, 63, 64, 65, 66, 68, 146, 147, 148, 149, 154, 155, 156, 157, 158, 159, 162, 163, 164, 165, 192, 193, 194, 195

Jean Randazzo: pages 36, 37 (both images), 42 (all images), 43, 54, 55, 223, 225, 235, 248, 249, 258, 259, 260, 262, 263, 264, 265, 266, 267

Jessica Shokrian: page 4

Tim Street Porter: pages 40, 41, 84, 85, 96 (bottom right), 108, 109, 221, 224, 226, 227, 246, 247

Robert Trachtenberg: pages 79, 82. 87. 178, 179, 244, 245

Simon Upton: pages 104, 150, 151, 152, 153, 160, 161, 243, 261

Miguel Flores-Vianna: pages 35, 38, 48, 49 (bottom right), 56, 57, 58-9, 75, 76-7, 78, 80-81, 83, 86, 88, 89, 92, 93, 94, 95, 102, 103, 105, 106 (all images), 107, 118, 119, 120, 121, 126 (bottom), 128, 129, 130, 131, 132, 133, 134, 135, 136, 137, 138, 139, 140, 141, 142, 143, 144, 145, 167, 176, 177, 180 (all images), 181, 182, 183, 184, 185, 186, 187, 188, 189, 190, 191, 196, 197, 198, 199, 200, 201, 205, 206, 207, 208, 209, 210, 211, 212 (all), 213, 214, 215, 216, 217, 218, 219), 238, 239, 240, 241, 242, 254, 255

Coral Von Zumwalt: page 124

Dominique Vorillon: pages 96 (top left), 97, 98, 99, 100, 101, 110, 111, 112, 113, 169

Courtesy of *Veranda*: pages 56, 57, 58-59, 61, 63, 64, 65, 66-67, 69, 167, 176-177, 180-181, 182-183, 184-185, 186-187, 188-189, 190-191, 196-197, 198-199, 200-201, 202-203, 207, 208-209, 210-211, 212-213, 214-215, 216-217, 218-219

First published in
the United States of America in 2010
by Rizzoli International Publications, Inc.
300 Park Avenue South
New York, NY 10010
www.rizzoliusa.com

© 2009 Mary McDonald

2010 2011 2012 2013 / 10 9 8 7 6 5 4 3 2 1

Distributed in the U.S. trade by Random House, New York

Printed in Singapore

ISBN-13: 978-0-8478-3393-1

Library of Congress Catalog Control Number: 2010927314

Art Direction: Doug Turshen with David Huang

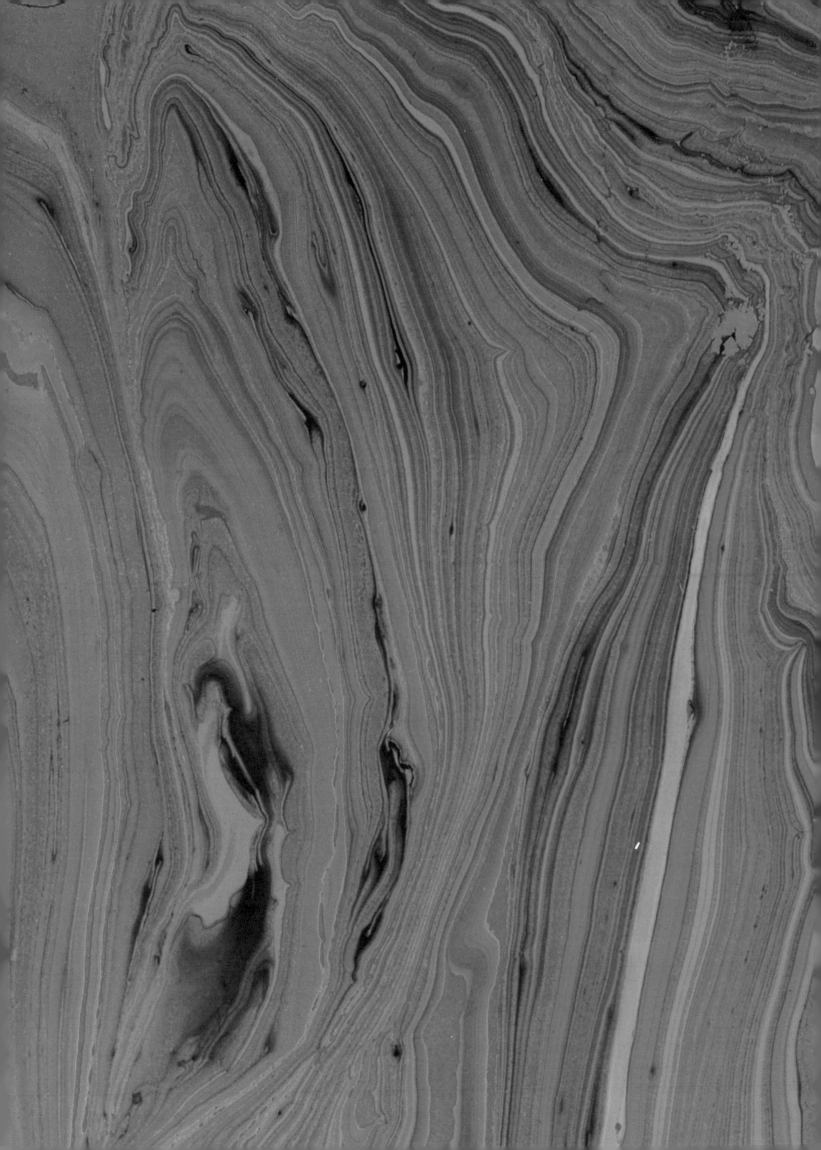